The Change[22]

Insights into Self-Empowerment

Jim Britt ~ Jim Lutes

With

Co-authors From Around the World

The Change[22]

Jim Britt ~ Jim Lutes

The Change

10556 Combie Road, Suite 6205

Auburn, CA 95602

Jim Lutes ~ Jim Britt

The Change Volume 22

ISBN#

Authors

Jim Britt

Jim Lutes

Kristi Mallory

Dr Louise Swartswalter

Helen Eimers

Melissa Barnes

Ryan Herpin

Jessica Rice

Michal Ofer

Patrick Richard Garcia

Dr. Yolanda Davis

Tina K Kailea

B. Von Squires

Angie Carlson

Vivian Shapiro

Stephanie Brandolini

Daniel Erbe

Lynn McIntosh

Daphne Paras

Steve Worme

Crystal Robinson

DEDICATION

To all those who dedicate their life to helping others live a more fulfilled life

PREFACE

By Jim Britt

One of the World's top 20 life and success strategists and top 50 most influential keynote speakers

The only constant in life is change. It swirls around us, weaving through the fabric of our existence, shaping our perspectives, molding our characters, and pushing us toward personal growth. Yet, despite its inevitability, change often comes with a veil of uncertainty and fear. How do we navigate these turbulent waters of transformation? How do we harness its power not only to survive, but to thrive?

"The Change-*Insights into self-empowerment*" is a collective journey into the heart of transformation, a treasury of wisdom from twenty-two diverse voices, each offering a unique perspective on self-empowerment. This anthology is more than a collection of essays; it is a tapestry of experiences, woven together to inspire, guide, and empower readers on their own paths of change.

As the co-creator and publisher of this anthology series, my journey began with a simple question: What does it truly mean to empower oneself in the face of change? The answers unfolded through the secrets and strategies shared by our esteemed coauthors. The depth of their insights reflects the rich tapestry of human experience, and their stories serve as both a mirror and a roadmap for those seeking self-empowerment.

The twenty-two chapters in this book are a testament to the resilience of the human spirit. Each coauthor generously shares their personal journey of transformation, offering glimpses into the moments of struggle, self-discovery and triumph. These writings are as diverse as the coauthors themselves, spanning over thirty countries, cultures, and life experiences. Yet, in their diversity, a common thread emerges—a shared commitment to embracing as a catalyst for personal empowerment.

Within these pages you'll discover several facets of the self-empowerment journey. "Awakening" is where our coauthors explore the pivotal moments that sparked their awareness and sparked their desire for change. Their stories demonstrate the transformative power of self-awareness, the first step on your own path to empowerment.

Next is "Resilience" where you can delve into the challenges our coauthors faced and the strength, they found within to overcome diversity. Whether dealing with loss, facing unexpected detours, or navigating the complexities of personal relationships, or in business, these stories illustrate the transformative nature of resilience and the inherent power within us to adapt and persevere.

Next, you'll find "Empowerment" which is the celebration of the intentional choices made by our coauthors to take charge of their lives. Through conscious decisions, mindset shifts, and a commitment to personal growth, they found the keys to unlocking their true potential. These stories and insights serve as beacons of inspiration for readers seeking to actively shape their own destinies.

And finally, "Integration" as our coauthors reflect on the ongoing journey of self-discovery and personal change. They share their practices, philosophies, and lessons that continue to guide them as they navigate the ever-changing landscape of life. These stories offer a roadmap for readers to integrate and sustain their newfound empowerment into their daily lives.

"The Change" is an invitation to explore the depths of your own potential, to embrace the certainty of change with open arms, and to recognize that within every challenge lies an opportunity for growth. It's a guide for those who seek not to just survive change but to harness its transformative power for a more empowered and fulfilling life overall.

So, as you embark on the journey through the pages of this volume of "The Change" I encourage you to approach each chapter with an open heart and curious mind, realizing that just one good idea acted upon can profoundly change your life. Let the stories and strategies shared by our coauthors be a source of inspiration, guidance, and confirmation that you too possess the power to navigate change with grace and determination and emerge stronger on the other side.

May this anthology serve as beacon of light, illuminating the path of self-empowerment and inspiring you to embrace the infinite possibilities that arise when you courageously and openly welcome change into your life.

With Gratitude and anticipation! Look forward to hearing your success story!

Jim Britt

http://JimBritt.com

FOREWORD

By Les Brown

Many of us spend at least a good part of our day going over internal dialog. We relive past experiences, worry about the future, blame the outside world for our shortcomings and criticize ourselves for not having all we want by this point in our lives. We do this both consciously and unconsciously. Even while we are listening to others, we aren't fully present. Instead, we are rehearsing our answers, slipping back into yesterday and worrying about tomorrow.

We live in uncertain times. We all feel we have minimum control over being able to change external circumstances, but we do have control over being able to change our internal environment, not only being able to see the truth behind a given situation but also how we respond to it. And to get the best out of the most stressful times, we need to demand the best from ourselves.

Many feel the pain of unhappiness. So many suffer from it daily, unaware that they can eliminate their suffering and find happiness by simply seeing the truth behind their unhappiness and making the right choices to change it. The problem is that our emotional conflicts are so familiar to us that they keep us blinded to better possibilities. We actually become addicted to feeling the way we do, thinking that it is just the way things are and we resign ourselves to getting by and coping.

I have had the privilege of speaking for over forty years serving millions of people from over 51 different countries. I know that there are certain patterns that create success and other patterns that breed internal conflict and failures.

The secret to being fulfilled and living the life you want is having the courage to go beyond the skills you've learned and discover the gifts that you were born with and to implement them daily. So many people settle for less in life, but I can tell you from my experience that it doesn't have to be that way.

I was born in an abandoned building on the floor with my twin brother in a poor section in Miami Florida called Liberty City. When we were six weeks of age, we were adopted by Mrs. Mimi Brown.

Whenever I speak, I always say that all that I am and all I ever hope to be I owe to my mother.

When I was in the fifth grade, I was labeled educable mentally retarded and put back from the fifth grade to the fourth grade and failed again when I was in the eighth grade. Mrs. Mimi Brown took my brother and I and five other kids in as foster kids and eventually adopted us.

Because of the work that Jim Britt does and the methods and techniques he uses to change your story and how you see yourself, it enabled me to build my career to make it against all odds. Both Jim Britt and Jim Lutes are icons in personal development and empowering others to be the best they can be.

You have something special inside. You have greatness in you. When you read this book, it will take you on a journey and introduce you to a part of yourself that has remained hidden and you didn't know existed.

When you begin to look at your goals and dreams realize that you have greatness inside you. "The Change" will provide the insights and processes of self-development that will empower you to manifest your greatness.

Jim Britt and I actually started the foundation of our speaking careers in the same direct selling company, Bestline, over 40 years ago. Although I haven't followed Jim Britt's career over the years, I do know that he is recognized as one of the top thought leaders in the world, helping millions of people create prosperous lives, rewarding relationships and spiritual awareness. He has authored 15 books and multiple programs showing people how to understand their hidden abilities to do more, become more and enjoy more in every area of life.

Today, Jim Britt and mind programming expert, Jim Lutes, along with inspiring co-authors from around the world, bring a pioneering work "The Change" book series to the market to transform lives. Their principles are forged on touching millions on every continent. As you read, you are exploring self-empowerment principles from a whole different perspective. In fact, Jim and Jim's publications of The Change book series now has hundreds of coauthors in 26 countries. The real power in each book is that 20 coauthors share their inspiring story so that the reader may benefit from their experience. It is packed with life-changing ideas, stories, tips, strategies on various empowering topics that you will love.

The principles, concepts and ideas within this book are sometimes simple, but can be profound to a person who is ready for that perfect message at the right time and is willing to take action to change. Maybe for one it's a chapter on relationships or leadership. For the next maybe it's a chapter on forgiveness or health awareness, and for another a simple life-changing message like I received as a youngster from a teacher. Each chapter is like opening a surprise empowering gift.

As I travel the world presenting my seminars, I meet people who spend more time and energy focused on what's wrong with society and their lives than is spent on helping each other improve the quality of life. With so much time spent on social media we often fear intimate contact with each other. Mistrust is often our first reaction. We judge and sometimes brutalize those among us who are in any way different from ourselves. We become addicted to anything that allows us a brief consolidation from the terrible pain we feel inside.

We need to begin to understand more about ourselves and our condition if there is ever to be the possibility of a healthy society. I believe this is possible and that's why I am so passionate about the work I do. Simply put…we are at war with ourselves. Real healing only takes place when we are willing to experience and face the truth within.

The conclusion to me is an exciting one. You, me and every other human being are shaping our brains and bodies by the thoughts we think, the emotions we feel, the intentions we hold, and the actions we take daily. Why is it exciting? Because we are in control of all these things and we can change as long as we have the intention, willingness and commitment to look inside, take charge of our lives and make the changes.

Whether you're pursuing, your dreams as an entrepreneur, a business owner or you want a more fulfilling relationship, or simply want to live a happy life, being authentic and actively appreciating what you're really capable of is going to be one of the most important assets you possess. It will make the difference between just "getting by" and really thriving and experiencing happiness or internal conflict.

Self-knowledge provides you with the emotional edge that will help you create a better life not only for yourself, but also for everyone with whom you come in contact.

This is the time to extract the best out of yourself and to use that gift to touch the lives of others.

I want to congratulate Jim Britt and Jim Lutes for making this publication series available and for allowing me to write the foreword. I honor them both and the coauthors within this book and the series for the lives they are changing.

As you enter these pages, do so slowly and with an open mind. Savor the wisdom you discover here, and then with interest and curiosity discover what rings true for you, and then take action toward the life you want.

Be prepared…because your life is about to change.

Hope to meet you one day at one of my seminars. And remember, everything you do counts!

Les Brown

Table of Contents

<This page is intentionally left blank>

Jim Britt

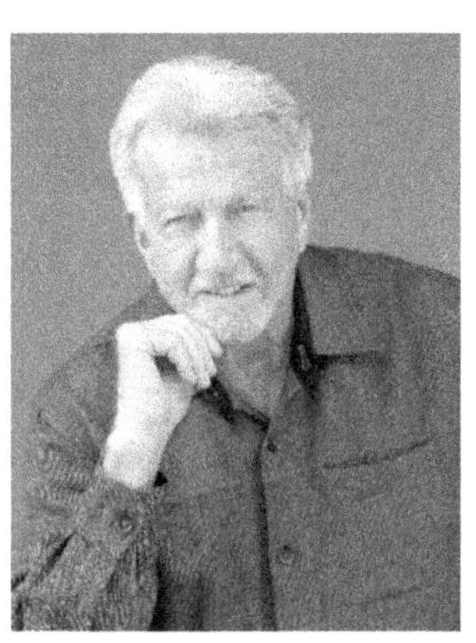

Jim Britt is an award-winning author of 15 best-selling books and fourteen #1 International best-sellers. Some of his many titles include Rings of Truth, Do This. Get Rich-For Entrepreneurs, Unleashing Your Authentic Power, The Power of Letting Go, Cracking the Rich Code and The Entrepreneur.

He is an internationally recognized business and life strategist who is highly sought after as a keynote speaker, both online and live, for all audiences.

As an entrepreneur Jim has launched 28 successful business ventures. He has served as a success strategist to over 300 corporations worldwide and was recently named as one of the world's top 50 speakers and top 20 success coaches. He was presented with the "Best of the Best" award out of the top 100 contributors of all time to the Direct Selling industry.

For over four decades Jim has presented seminars throughout the world sharing his success strategies and life enhancing realizations with over 5,000 audiences, totaling almost 2,000,000 people from all walks of life.

Early in his speaking career he was Business partners with the late Jim Rohn for eight years, where Tony Robbins worked under Jim's direction for his first few years in the speaking business.

As a performance strategist, Jim leverages his skills and experience as one of the leading experts in peak performance, entrepreneurship and personal empowerment to produce stellar results. He is pleased to work with small business entrepreneurs, and anyone seeking to remove the blocks that stop their success in any area of their life.

One of Jim's latest programs "Cracking the Rich Code" focuses on the subconscious programs influencing one's relationship with money and their financial success. www.CrackingTheRichCode.com

Think Like Superman

By Jim Britt

"Waking up to your true greatness in life requires letting go of who you imagine yourself to be."

--- Jim Britt

FACT: Becoming a millionaire is easier than it has ever been.

Many people have the notion that it's an impossible task to become a millionaire. Some say, "It's pure luck." Others say, "You have to be born into a rich family." For others, "You'll have to win the Lotto." And for many they say, "Your parents have to help you out a lot." That's the language of the poor.

A single mother with five children says, "I want to believe in what you're saying. However, I'm 45 years old and work long hours at two dead-end jobs. I barely earn enough to get by. What should I do?"

Another man said, "Well, if you work for the government, you cannot expect to become a millionaire. After all, you're on a fixed salary and there's little time for anything else. By the time you get home, you've got to play with the kids, eat dinner, and fall asleep watching TV."

Everyone has a story as to why they could never become a millionaire. But for every story, excuse really, there are other stories OR PEOPLE with worse circumstances, that have become rich.

The truth is that all of us can become as wealthy as we decide to be, and that's a mindset. None of us is excluded from wealth. If you have the desire to receive money, whatever the amount, you have all of the rights to do so like everyone else. There is no limit to how much you can earn for yourself. The only limitations are what you place on yourself.

Money is like the sun. It does not discriminate. It doesn't say, "I will not give light and warmth to this flower, tree, or person because I don't like them." Like the sun, money is abundantly available to all of us who truly believe that it is for us. No one is excluded.

There are, however, some major differences between rich and poor people. Here are some tips for becoming rich.

Change Your Thinking

You have to see the bigger picture. There are opportunities everywhere! The problem is that most people see just trees, when they should be looking at the entire forest. By doing so you will see that there are opportunities everywhere. The possibilities are endless.

You'll also have to go through plenty of self-discovery before you earn your first million. Knowing the truth about yourself isn't always the easiest task. Sometimes, you'll find that you are your biggest enemy—at least some days.

Learn from Millionaires

Most people are surrounded by what I like to call their "default friends." These friends are acquaintances that we see at the gym, school, work, local happy hour, and other places. We naturally befriend these people because we are all in the same boat financially. However, in most cases, these people aren't millionaires and cannot help you become one either. In fact, if you tell them you are going to become a millionaire, some may even tell you that it's impossible and discourage you from even trying. They'll tell you that you're living in a fantasy world and why you'll never be able to make it happen. Instead, learn from millionaires. Let go of these relationships that pull you down when it comes to your money desires. It's okay to have friends that aren't millionaires. However, only take input from those that have accomplished what you want to accomplish. Hang out with those that will encourage and help you get to the next level. Don't give your raw diamonds to a brick layer to be cut.

Indulge in Wealth

To become wealthy, you must learn about wealth. This means that you'll have to put yourself in situations that you've never been in before.

ON OCCASION, DO SOME OF THESE:

Fly first class and see how it makes you feel.

Eat out at the finest restaurant and don't look at the price.

Take a limo instead of a cab or Uber. Watch how you feel.

Reserve a suite in a first-class hotel.

If you are used to drinking a $20 bottle of wine, go for the $100 and see how it tastes. It does taste different.

All I am saying is, try some of the things that wealthy people do and see how it makes you feel.

Believe it is Possible

If you believe that it is possible to become a millionaire, you can make it happen. However, if you've excluded yourself from this possibility and think and believe that it's for other people, you'll never become a millionaire.

Also, be sure to bless rich people when you can. Haters of money aren't likely to receive any of it either.

Read books that have been written by millionaires. By gaining a well-rounded education about earning large sums of money and staying inspired, you'll be able to learn the wealth secrets of the rich. I just saw a video on LinkedIn with my friend Kevin Harrington from the TV show Shark Tank. He said that one of his new companies just had a million-dollar day on Amazon.

Enlarge Your Service

Your material wealth is the sum of your total contribution to society. Your daily mantra should be, *'How do I deliver more value to more people in less time?'* Then, you'll know that you can always increase your quality and quantity of service. Enlarging your service is also about going the extra mile. When it comes to helping others, you must give it everything you have. You just plant the seeds and nature will take care of the rest.

Seize ALL Opportunities That Make Sense

You cannot say "No" to opportunities and expect to become a millionaire. You must seize every opportunity that has your name on it. It may just be an opportunity to connect with an influential person for no reason. Sometimes the monetary reward will not come immediately, but if you keep planting seeds, eventually you'll grow a fruitful crop. Money is the harvest of the service you provide and sometimes the connections you have. The more seeds you plant, the greater the harvest.

Have an Unstoppable Mindset

Want to know some of what my first mentor shared with me that took me from a broke factory worker, high school dropout, to millionaire?

First, he said, you have to start thinking like a wealthy, unstoppable person. You have to have a wealth mindset. He said that wealthy people think differently. He said, "I want you to start thinking like Superman!" Sounds crazy, right? Well, it's not. It's powerful and here's why. How you think will change your life.

Wealthy people think differently. They really do. And anyone can learn to think like the wealthy.

I'm not talking about positive thinking, Law of Attraction, or motivation. Let's get real. None of that stuff works anyway. Otherwise, we would all be rich and happy already. I'm talking about thinking based in quantum physics science. Once you understand and apply it, it will change your life. You will become unstoppable!

If there was any person, fictional or real, whose qualities you could instantly possess, who would that person be? Think about it. Personally, I would say that Superman is the perfect person. Now, you are probably thinking I have lost it right? Just stick with me here. I think you will like what you are about to hear.

Superman is a fictional superhero widely considered to be one of the most famous and popular action hero and an American cultural icon. I remember watching Superman every Saturday morning when I was a kid. I couldn't get enough. He was my hero!

Let's look at Superman's traits:

Superman is indestructible.

He is a man of steel.

He can stop a locomotive in its tracks.

Bullets bounce off him.

He is faster than a speeding bullet.

No one can bring him down.

He can leap tall buildings in a single bound. Great powers to have in this day-and-age, wouldn't you say? What else would you need?

Now, for all you females, don't worry, we have not left you out. There is also a female version of Superman, named Superwoman. She has the same powers as Superman.

Now, this is where it gets interesting. Let's first look at the qualities that Superman possesses that you want to make your own. And to make it simple, I will refer to Superman for the rest of this message, and you can replace with Superwoman if you are female.

Again:

Superman is powerful and fearless.

Superman is virtually indestructible—except for kryptonite of course.

Superman can stop bullets.

Superman has supernatural powers. He can see through walls.

Superman can stop a speeding locomotive.

Superman can stop a bullet.

Superman jumps into immediate action when troubles arise.

Superman can crash through barriers.

Superman can even change clothes in a phone booth in seconds. Not too many of those around anymore. You'll have to duck behind a building to change.

So, you're thinking right now, *'Ok, I know that Superman has incredible supernatural powers, how can that help me? What good will it do me to think I am Superman, a fictional character?'*

Here is where science comes in. This is the part where you will be amazed when you learn about the supernatural powers that you already possess! NO, REALLY!

Your brain makes certain chemicals called neuro peptides. These are literally the molecules of emotion, like love, fear, joy, passion, and so on. These molecules of emotion are not only contained in your brain they actually circulate throughout your cellular structure. They send out a signal, a frequency much like a radio station sending out a signal. For example, you tune to 92.5 and you get jazz. Tune to 99.6 and you get rock. And if you are just one decimal off, you get static. The difference is that your signal goes both ways. You are a sender and a receiver.

You put out a signal, a mindset, of confidence about your financial success and people, circumstances, and opportunities show up to support your success. When you put out a signal of doubt and uncertainty and you receive support for your doubt and uncertainty. You've been around someone that you didn't trust, or you felt less than positive just being in their presence, right? You have also been around people that inspire you. That's what I'm talking about. You are projecting a frequency, looking to resonate with the frequency you are transmitting.

Anyway, the amazing part about these cells of emotion is that they are intelligent. They are thinking cells. These cells are constantly eavesdropping on the conversation that you are having with yourself. That's right. They are listening to you! And others are listening to your cells as well. Others feel what you feel when they are around you.

Your unconscious mind, your cells, are listening in, waiting to adjust your behavior based on what they hear from you, their master. So just imagine what would happen if you started to think like Superman…or like a millionaire.

Here are some of the thoughts you might have during the day:

"The challenges I face day today are easily overcome, after all I am Superman."

"I am indestructible."

"I have incredible strength."

"Nothing can stop me.....NOTHING."

"I have supernatural powers and can overcome anything."

"I can accomplish anything I want when I put my mind to it."

"I can break through any barrier."

"I can and I will do whatever it takes to accomplish my goal."

"I fear nothing."

The trillions of thinking cells in your body and brain listen, and they create exactly what you tell them to create. Their mission is to complete the picture of the you they see and hear when you talk to them. They must obey. It's their job!

Since you are Superman, you cannot fail. Why? Your thinking cells are now sending out the right signal, because you told them to. They are making you stronger, more successful, every day! You have the ability to fight off all negativity, doubt, fear, and worry—nothing can stop you!

Superman has total confidence. So, your cells of emotion relating to confidence will now create more neuro peptide chemicals to promote feelings of power and confidence that others will feel in your presence.

Superman is fearless. So, your cells of emotion relating to fear will now create more neuro peptide chemicals to create feelings of courage. You are unstoppable!

And here's the key. Others will respond to you in the same way that you are talking to yourself.

If you are confident, others will have confidence in you.

You have thousands of thoughts every day. Make sure your thoughts are leading you in the direction you want to go. Make sure you are telling your cells a success story, and not a 'woe is me' story.

Most have been conditioned to think that creating wealth is difficult, or that it's only for the lucky few. What do you believe? It doesn't cost you any more to think like Superman; and it's much more inspiring!

Mediocrity cannot be an option if you decide to be wealthy and think like Superman.

Your decision, and communication with your cells, creates a mindset; that mindset influences how you show up.

None of that old type of thinking matters anymore…after all, you are Superman, and you can accomplish anything.

If you want wealth, you have to stretch yourself. You have to do the things that unsuccessful people are not willing to do. You have to say "yes" to opportunity, then figure out how to get the job done.

Maybe you are uncomfortable selling and asking for money. If that's the case, then learn sales and learn to ask for money every day until you feel comfortable asking for it. You will never have money if you don't learn to ask for it.

I've learned a lot in the past 40+ years as an entrepreneur. I've learned that in order to have more, you have to become more. I've also learned that if you are comfortable, you are not growing. I learned that I couldn't go from a nervous rookie speaker with minimal self-confidence to hosting TV shows and speaking in front of 5,000 people overnight. I simply wasn't ready. I grew into that, one speaking engagement at a time. Every time I finished a speaking engagement, I would ask myself, "How did I do, and how could I do it better?" I still do that today.

And I've learned from the hundreds of thousands of people I've trained, coached, and mentored that none of us can do something we don't believe is possible. It's not going to happen if you're not ready to step out of your comfort zone and stretch yourself.

This has led me to understand the single most important principle of wealth-building, that has meant the difference between poverty and riches for people since humans first traded for pelts.

Are you ready?

Come in just a little closer. Listen up!

Every income level requires a different you, a different mindset! If you think that $10,000 a month is a lot of money, then $100,000 a month will be completely out of reach. If you believe that having $5,000 in the bank would make you rich, then $50,000 won't miraculously appear. You will never earn more money than you believe is "a lot" of money.

What you do as a business is only a small part of becoming rich. In fact, there are thousands, if not tens of thousands, of ways to make money—and lots of it. What I've learned over the years is that, by focusing on who you want to become instead of what you need to do, you're going to multiply your chances of getting rich a hundred-fold.

Ask anyone who's found a way to make a large sum of money legally, and he or she will tell you that it's not hard once you crack the code. And cracking the code starts with you and your mindset. The "code" to which I refer isn't a secret rite or ancient scroll. It's not even a secret. It's a certain way of thinking and believing in which you've trained your mind to see money-making ideas.

That's where you see a need in the marketplace, and you jump on the idea quickly. It might involve creating a new product; or, it may just be teaching others a special technique you've learned. It may even require raising capital to start a company or to market a product or idea on social media.

Don't Hold Back. You Have to Take Action to Change.

Start right now to imagine yourself as already having wealth. How would your life be? How would your day unfold? Start to own your wealth mindset now! The subconscious mind is unable to differentiate between actual fact and mere visualization. So, by imagining that you already have it, you're encouraging your subconscious mind to seek the ways and means to transform your imaginary feelings into the real thing.

Find yourself some mentors. Nobody has all the answers. Surround yourself with people that will support, inspire, and provide you with answers that keep you moving in the right direction. If you truly want to attain wealth, have a thriving business, or reach the top of your game in any endeavor, having a qualified mentor is essential.

Okay, lets come in for a landing …

It is absolutely essential to have a crystal-clear picture of what you want to accomplish before you begin. If you want to attain wealth, you must learn to operate without fear and with a sharply defined mental image of the outcome you want to attain. This comes from thinking like a wealthy person, (like Superman) making decisions like a wealthy person and being fearless (like Superman) when it comes to stepping out of your comfort zone. Look at the end result as something you're already prepared to do, you just haven't done it yet.

Think about this. Your success is something that you have been preventing; it's not something you have to struggle to make happen. The key is to not let fear, doubt, other people, or mind chatter push your success away. You'll find that the solutions taking you toward your goals will come to you in the most unexpected and sudden ways. You don't need the *perfect* plan first. What you need is a perfectly clear decision about your success, the right mindset, the right mentoring, and the ideal way to get you there will materialize.

The greatest transfer of wealth in the history of the human race is happening right now. Are you positioned to get your share?

Remember, in order to get a different result, you must do something different. In order to do something different you must know something different to do. And in order to know something different, you have to first suspect that your present methods need improving.

THEN, YOU HAVE TO BE WILLING TO DO SOMETHING ABOUT IT.

***

For more information on Jim's work:

www.JimBritt.com

http://JimBrittCoaching.com

www.facebook.com/jimbrittonline

www.linkedin.com/in/jim-britt

For free audio series www.RichCode1.com and www.RichCode2.com

http://becomeAcoauthor.com

To find out how to crack the rich code and change your subconscious programming regarding your relationship with money: www.CrackingTheRichCode.com

Jim Lutes

Say the name Jim Lutes and chances are a top performer in your company has attended one or more of his dynamic trainings over the last few years.

Having taught his branded form of human performance since the early 1990s, Mr. Lutes has accelerated top level entrepreneurs throughout his career by conducting training on personal growth and subconscious programming into worldwide markets.

During this time Jim took his skills regarding the human mind, and combining it with training on influence, persuasion and communication strategies he launched Lutes International in the early 1990s. Based in San Diego California Jim has taught seminars for, corporations, sales forces, individuals and athletes. Having appeared on television, radio and worldwide stages, Jim's style, knowledge and effectiveness provide profound results.

"Jim Lutes possesses a unique ability to create performance change in an individual in a fraction of the time it takes his competitors". The core of human decisions is based on the programs we acquire, reinforce and grow. Combining Jims various trainings individuals can reach new levels of achievement and fulfillment in all areas of life. The results are at times nothing short of astonishing.

"My goal is to take that embryonic greatness that exists inside every person in America, foster it, empower it and then hand them personal strategies based on solid principles that allow them to take that new attitude and apply it to creating a life masterpiece".

What You do with YOU

By Jim Lutes

Most people think that if they can just learn enough, earn enough, get smart enough, then they will BE enough. And they think that when that happens, they can finally relax and be happy. But what happens is that they get so caught up in what they are constantly *doing* that are not focused on how they are *being*.

In other words, they are not focused on their emotional state. When you engage your emotions, your subconscious mind begins to get the messages and begins to establish new rules and new behaviors. Then, it becomes a way of life and enters your heart and really begins to come from your heart. When it is in your heart then it is truly part of you. When you are really getting it at the deepest level, is when you can begin to anticipate what I am going to say, you know you understand it at a much deeper level right now.

I began to study human performance as a way to make some changes in my own life and when I began to see some serious results, I got so excited about it that I wanted to share it with other people. So I committed my life to learning and sharing what works with others. So, I am a committed lifetime learner and therefore I have been fortunate enough to have had the ability to look at and study just about every approach there is to personal development and success that is available in today's market. I am a strong advocate of clear, simple, workable approaches that get dependable and lasting results.

Because of the vast wealth of information my Life Masterpiece teaching gives you and the amazing results you will get, you will likely find yourself returning to it again and again throughout your life.

No matter how successful we are, or how successful we become, we all need a coach to encourage us, to challenge us, to remind us to live up to our potential. I am going to be here to do that for you each day, and it is both my honor and my privilege to serve you in that way.

Let's get started now.

The person that you are, and that person that you must become in order to put the colors of your life masterpiece where you want them and blend them in just the right combination to create your own unique experience might right now seem like two very different people, but they are one in the same. You are that person right now. I am going to help you uncover your true identity and purpose so that you can then activate the universal laws and make them work for you.

When we let go of all the stories, we have been telling ourselves about who we think we are supposed to be and what we think we are supposed to do and have, we not only free ourselves we free our families, our children, our intimate partners, and our friends in the process. There is no way you can make a difference in yourself without touching somebody else even if it is not your intention.

The Life Masterpiece focus is about what you can do with YOU. If you want to change any circumstance, any relationship, then you must begin with yourself no matter how convinced you are that somebody else or something else must change. Changing yourself can change even the most rigid system and stubborn person. And ANY progress moves you forward. And any movement forward on your part creates the opportunity for every other part of your life to be moved forward as well.

One of the most effective ways for you to reprogram your mind is through what I like to call vicarious experiences. These are the experiences other people have had and I will bring you through their experiences by sharing their stories with you. These stories are not in this book simply to fill it up and make it fat like you find in some books. These stories are the heart and soul of the book because this is how you will begin to reprogram your subconscious and take the information into your heart where it will transform you.

The reason why vicarious experiences are so powerful is because they relate to you and so when you are reading these stories your conscious mind will get go and your unconscious mind will get the lesson.

And when you read some of these remarkable stories and meet some of these people who have gone through some amazing personal transformations, you will begin to realize that no matter who you are, no matter what part of the world you are from or what culture you grew up in, whether you grow up poor, wealthy or somewhere in between, whether you grow up with religion or Monday Night Football, you will begin to realize that we all have the same problems.

So, what will happen is you will begin to connect with these people because they have the same problems you have- the same challenges. They are universal. You will then see what the reason is for this is that we all have the same basic needs, our lives are about meeting these needs and that they impact and determine every single thing we do and every decision we make.

Every single habit, behavior, rule or pattern is your unconscious way of trying to get your needs met. And your needs are the same exact needs every other human being on the planet has. We all use different behaviors to get these needs met but they are still the same.

Some of the behaviors we use are positive and healthy and some of them are not quite so resourceful. And this is one of the reasons why even though we all have the same needs and the same problems, we all get different results. We are hard wired with the same needs, but not with the same subconscious programming. And the reason why we all get different results boils down to one thing- standards.

You know, so often in life, we find ourselves in a position where we live life a certain way. We act a certain way. We were raised in a certain way. And through our lives in an effort to avoid pain and still meet our needs, we made critical decisions about who we are and how we think we need to be. And so we believe we know who we are.

But the way we have behaved for years is simply an *adaptation.* Something that happened in response to the desire we had to meet our basic needs- to get the love, or respect, or acceptance from a parent, lover, loved one or peers- caused us to make a key decision and adapt to the circumstances around us. We do not ever realize that for years we have been living something that we are really good at but which is not necessarily our true nature.

One of the things you will learn here is that a single decision has the power to change everything in a heartbeat. In fact, when you stay with me through this you are going to learn about a decision, I made perhaps some time ago that determines the choices you have made in the course of your life up until now. Today he made a decision to pick up this book and begin this journey with me and if you will indulge me for just a few hours the decision to pick up this book might be the decision that changes everything in your life from today on.

Now that you've made the decision to read it, I will tell you what this book can really do for you. It will get you to uncover and maybe for the first time really identify how the role models of your life have affected your subconscious decision-making in ways you never dreamed possible.

Without getting into the actual science behind it, a child's brain works much differently than an adult brain. As you might already know our brains operate using four different wavelengths -- alpha, beta, theta and delta. Most of the time, the adult brain operates at the beta level when we are awake. The beta level is when our eyes are focused in our conscious mind is in control, and we are logical. The alpha level is a level that we must pass through to go to sleep and to wake up, and it's also the most common level is one we are in a trance. Theta is for a deeper trance or dreaming, and delta is for deep sleep.

This means that when we are at the alpha level, we are highly impressionable, because the messages are going directly into our subconscious minds. A child's mind is different because it operates primarily at the alpha level, which is why children are so impressionable. This also means that our parents and other significant people in our childhood had a tremendous impact on the messages that are subconscious mind received and events from our childhood had a strong impact on our self-image, our identity and how we develop as adults. This is why when we speak about reprogramming the subconscious mind is very important to talk about her childhood and her relationship with her parents. This is not done to point fingers or place blame, but to help us understand some of the reasons for the choices that we make for the patterns that we keep repeating and how they carry over from generation to generation.

Even if you feel like you held your own when you were growing up, and that the relationships that you had as a child -- especially the relationship she had with your mother and father -- were strong, and you feel like you are strong as a result. There are still patterns that your subconscious mind is running that no longer serve you. Because it's the tension, the experience of having to deal with all of the events of your past and even the events that happened before you were born in your parent's past -- all of these experiences affect your decision making, your relationships, your finances, your choices, behaviors and life circumstances, even today.

Even if your childhood was perfect and you feel like you honor, respect and love your parents and adore all of your siblings and even if your parents or your greatest role models, you are still affected on many levels and in many ways. And because you decided to read this book, I believe you have some things you would like to change. If you change anything, first you must learn to reprogram your subconscious mind and part of doing so is to understand that the key decisions you made in the past still impact you today.

Our childhood role models deeply affect both our conscious and subconscious decision-making and behavior patterns. We are all examples, and some of us are warnings. We all, at one time or another, impact other people. This is one of the reasons why I stress that it is so important to live consciously and be an example.

When I ask people about their belief systems and the habits and patterns that basically control their lives, I am often struck by how few of these beliefs and habits were ever chosen by that person on a conscious level. In other words, the rules that are guiding your life about how to BE in your own life very often picked up unconsciously.

It is incredible how common it is that people start this process, and when they begin to reassess their lives and their relationships with themselves and others in the success they are having or perhaps not having, they discover that much of what has been screwing up their lives, their achievements, their finances, their careers, their intimate relationships, and even their bodies (and I am not talking about the excuse many of us use about genetics. Being the reason, our bodies look the way they do) was influenced by their PARENTS. Not by their parents' problems necessarily, but by somehow trying to be liked, loved or appreciated by one parent. Many times, these decisions also have to do with trying to avoid pain that was inflicted by a parent or other significant role model, or simply standing up to a parent.

We can be 40, 50 or even 80 years old, and we are still living the strategies of a child.

And what's even worse, is it very often when we were a kid, we said, "I'll never be like that!" And here you are today, exactly like that! You don't want to admit it but if you held up a mirror and watched a film of your interactions you would say, "Oh my God, I never wanted to be like that parent." And yet you are. Or perhaps you have done the opposite. Perhaps you have thrown the pendulum the other way and you're not like that parent at all. Now, you are something worse. Or, let's just say you are something else. You are the opposite of the extreme you didn't like. And so now you are another extreme, that doesn't work either. Because no one teaches us this stuff, and so it becomes unconscious. We don't even see it. It's part of the invisible fabric of our thinking and our decision-making every single day.

This book will give you a unique opportunity to look deep inside yourself. It will allow you to look inside of your relationships, your decisions about money, and your decisions about your career, your relationship with God or your higher power, and even your body. It will allow you to understand how your own up bringing us may be influenced you and you probably know a lot of the ways it has influenced you, but maybe you'll spot some of the decisions you have made, maybe even one core decision that has affected your identity.

So, what the heck does identity mean anyway? It can be such a big and often loaded word. Well, I believe identity is the strongest force in the human personality. If you want to know what shapes you the most it's not your capability. It's your identity and the rules you have for who you think you are.

And you know what the challenge is? Most of us defined ourselves a long time ago. And when we step outside that definition, we get uncomfortable, because the strongest force in the human personality is the need to remain consistent with how we define ourselves. Later, we will talk about the human needs referred to earlier. One of them is certainty. What this means is that if certainty is one of the deepest needs we have, then if you don't know who you are, you do not know how to act.

Very early in life, we begin to define who we are. We use labels such as loner, aggressive conservative, sexy, successful, loser, rich or poor.

I work for others. I am ugly. I am smart. I am a procrastinator. I am clumsy. I am athletic. I am thin. I am big boned. What happens is these definitions become self-fulfilling prophecies because nobody wants to be disappointed. Nobody wants to live in a place of uncertainty. So, there may be arranging your identity or in your definition of yourself, but it may not be absolute.

The metaphor that you so often hear what we talk about our comfort zone, is that our comfort zone is like a thermostat. We all have our comfort zone, and it is set by our subconscious mind. So, if your subconscious mind has set your thermostat in a particular area of your life, for example how much money you make, that let's say 45°, and if the temperature drops down to 40°, guess what happens? It doesn't meet your identity. In other words, things are not good enough, whether it be mentally and emotionally financially with your weight (which by the way is the primary reason people whose weight tend to gain it back because they lose it before reprogramming their subconscious mind to reset the thermostat) or whatever.

For example, if you drop down to 40° and your finances and 45° is your identity. This means that 45° is what you must have. Or, if you drop down to 70° in your intimacy and 80° is your identity, then this is what you must have. Whatever it is, when you drop below your comfort zone, you will be compelled to drive to make it better automatically. If your body gets out of control, there is a point at which you go, “that's enough!” You are willing to be a little off your identity but not that much. And suddenly you go on the diet suddenly make the change because you feel the pressure that comes with being inconsistent with your own definition of how you think you should be.

But what most of us fail to recognize is that this happens on the other side as well. Your subconscious mind since your mental thermostat at say 45° for your finances or 80° mentally for how close you want to be with your intimate partner, or 70° for how your body should look and feel,

This is not your *goal*. Your goal is something much larger. This is your subconscious comfort zone or your subconscious definition of yourself. For example, you might think of yourself as big boned, but if it suddenly isn't good enough and you really become overweight, then you change to fit your self-image or your definition of yourself in order to get back into that comfort zone. But also, if it gets better than you expected, perhaps, you lose a lot of weight and get really good shape, or perhaps you lead your company in sales for two quarters in a row when you normally come in third or fourth, or perhaps you jump from 70° in your intimacy, and now you have a relationship that is at 90 or even 100°. You have a really hot, passionate relationship with more passion than you ever have before, or you lose three dress sizes instead of one, or you double your income, whatever it is, your subconscious mind starts talking some sense into you. And your brain goes, "Hello, dude what the heck are you doing? You are 70 degree-er, what in heck are you doing way appear at 90? You can't keep that. That's not gonna last. Get back down to 70° before you get hurt or fail or screw it up. You're in over your head. You're not an entrepreneur. You work for other people."

Wherever your subconscious mind has set your comfort zone based on the way you define yourself, you're going to keep adjusting to stay in that comfort zone. So many times, in these types of programs, people challenge you to get out of your comfort zone, which you can't do consciously. You have to go into your subconscious and reset your comfort zone, just like you would the thermostat. And this will keep happening until you reprogram your subconscious mind with a new identity, and the new comfort zone. Before you set out to make any kind of lasting change, you must reset your subconscious comfort zone.

And what do we do when we exceed our comfort zone? Well, what happened is that the drive to make things better stops. And so you stop growing and gradually you drift back until you reach your comfort zone. Or worse, you start to sabotage. The mental air conditioners kick on and bring yourself right back down to where you think you deserve to be based on your subconscious identity.

For example, if the only kind of love you view as a child was abuse, the only kind of life. You knew was living paycheck to paycheck or in debt, or the only kind of lifestyle you ever experienced with sedentary, whatever it is, even though it might be painful. It is what you know. This becomes your comfort zone and therefore provides the certainty that you need. It becomes your self-definition and what you think you deserve. You begin to think -- not consciously, but unconsciously -- this IS love, this is just the body. You inherited, or that wealth is for other kinds of people, or you're not the right kind of person to make certain kinds of social contacts. Of course, this is not your conscious thinking that this is what is going on in your subconscious.

And therein lays the trouble, or perhaps a better way to say it, the shortcomings with many of the programs you may have tried in the past. They pump you up and felt good about it. They motivated you with affirmations and taught you to use visualization. They've even taught you that the universal laws work for everyone. You may have even made some changes, but they did not last. Because when you're taught these things, you know the stuff in your head on a conscious level. But your identity and self-definition is the thermostat of subconscious mind, so before you can make any substantive or lasting change, first you must reprogram your subconscious mind and change who you are at the deepest level. (Green papers).

In other words, you must become the kind of person who has whatever it is that you want. Visualizing it, affirming it, and even living your life by a new set of standards is not going to work long term until this stuff goes from your conscious to your unconscious and finally into your heart. Not only do you have to DO it, and not only do you have to LIVE it, but you also have to BECOME it. And then you will manifest it.

And that is the difference between the stick figure you are drawing now or the paint by numbers life you have been taught to lead and the masterpiece you are now creating. So, for the colors in our masterpiece is to really live consciously, to be an example, then we have to get conscious about what is shaping us and the thing that shapes you most identity.

Someone who is outrageous will behave, say things differently and move differently than someone who believes they are extremely conservative. They will use a different voice, a different way of moving and a different language. Here is my question for you:

When did you come up with this definition?

When did you decide who you are?

When was the last time you updated it?

Maybe it's time to take another look at who you are today. And maybe you don't have to actually give up your identity. Maybe the identity created for yourself is magnificent, but maybe it's time to expand it. Maybe it's time to add to it. Maybe it's time to open up to a new level of freedom and options.

And when you do that there will be a processional effect in all areas of your life, because we are all connected in a cybernetic loop. If I want to change you, I can try to control you, but that will not change anything. Or I can try to change the system, but that will not last or will be futile. Or I can change me into an ID so that everything changes.

For example, if I change the way I treat you, the way I respond to you, my voice my body my feelings and my emotions by respect for you. It will affect the way you feel and the way you respond back. And the same is true with the universe and higher intelligence. Once you change yourself, reprogram your subconscious, become the person you need to become that the things that you want in your life, then you will begin to receive a different response from the universe in a different result in your life. Then begin to experience your life as a masterpiece.

You will learn that what we value controls what we are willing to do or not do -- in our businesses, and our relationships, with our bodies and with our children. Some people get locked in place into a mindset. I call it being committed to your commitment. For example, have you ever been in an argument, and you were so angry that as the argument progressed, you forgot what you were angry about, and it just became about winning? We've all been there and what happens is we get committed to being angry and said that resolving the argument. Or we get committed to being right, instead of uncovering the truth. When this happens, get so wrapped up in our commitment that we can no longer see the forest through the trees. We lose touch with what we really want, because we get stuck in a mindset, and we get committed to our commitments.

(Judy- discovers a decision she made as a child and uses the discovery to transform her life and her children and grandchildren's lives).

Today, you are beginning a process that can truly change the quality of your life forever and can take that paint by numbers life you might be living now and create the masterpiece called your life. So just for a moment now, what I want you to do is imagine that your life is a painting. And imagine that you have died and are looking down at that painting. What did you leave behind? Is your life, a masterpiece that is cherished and hangs prominently as an example for others of what is possible, or is it a paint-by-numbers life that is packed away in someone's basement?

As you begin this process, I asked for only two things from you:

- Your heartfelt desire to make real changes.
- The commitment to follow through and do this, as simple or as located as it might seem in the moment.

If you can do just those two things, then the things that you used to call dreams will become part of your daily reality.

Why is it that you can have a person who seems to have superior abilities, talents, skills, and education, at the same time, they don't produce the quality of life they want or that you might expect from them? And why is it, on the other hand, you can have someone who seemingly has every disadvantage -- no family support, the wrong social status, no emotional support, no education, and the wrong background -- and yet they go out and produce results, way beyond what anyone could have expected or even imagined?

The difference in our quality of life is not about our capability, background or education. Human beings, *that means you*, are *all capable* of achieving incredible results, and yet sadly only a few seem to get it.

What people WILL do is very different from what people CAN do.

I want to challenge you right now to start using your WILL muscle, instead of your TRY muscle, which is probably overdeveloped anyhow. I challenge you to start exercising your inborn human power, which is your birthright as a member of the human race, your ability to act based on the choice and free will that every human has in equal measure. Frankly, this means that if it has been achieved, then there is no reason on earth why you cannot achieve it. And beyond that, if it can be imagined, then there is also very little reason why you cannot achieve it. As a matter of fact, your unconscious mind will rarely imagine something that you are capable of. That is the difference between desires and fantasies. It's true. There are no excuses anymore. If you are reading this and you are a human being that you have the ability to take action and to produce results.

The disability that I'm talking about is not something I can give you. Why? Because you already have it. You were born, great. Now, I challenge you to go out and take back what is rightfully yours.

Hopefully, something is now a weekend within you in two ways. One, by igniting your desire and two by showing you some simple systematic strategies on how you can get greater results on a daily basis.

When most of us think of success or failure, we tend to think of these monumental things. Failure is not an overnight thing, and neither is success.

Just what is success? Well, some people describe it in terms of achievements like a resume. But it is different for everyone. So, some people describe it as a feeling.

The truth is that success is wrapped up in failure. What I mean by that is that success is simply a string of failures all going in the same purposeful direction. That's right. If you want to find success you have to look inside a failure. In other words, if you want to be more successful than the next person, then you simply have to be willing to experience more failure, but not just any failures. You must be willing to take specific actions, based on specific decisions, that may fail most of the time, but keep going, perhaps with a new strategy, experience and more failures, and eventually you will succeed. If this sounds painful, then I want you to think for a moment about what true failure actually is.

True failure is lifelong failure. It is the failure of inactivity. It's not actually failing at what you DO -- those things will lead to success. But when you fail to DO, you fail to succeed. In failing to do is a recipe for ultimate failure in life. When you fail to make the calls, when you fail to follow through, when you fail to say I love you, when you fail to give your all, that is what creates the ultimate failure in life. Ultimate failure creates the greatest pain, the feelings we want to avoid at all costs. Now *that* is painful.

Success happens one step at a time. Success happens one failure at a time. It is successfully making the calls and doing it no matter how long it takes for the outcome in the moment. It is successfully getting up and following through. It is successfully making sure that you make that unique contact. It is successfully breaking through the limits that used to stop you.

Success is a combination of all those little things -- those little successes that often come disguised as failures -- over each day and over your lifetime that eventually create a life that you will have total pride and great joy in knowing that you created your life and made it into a masterpiece of your very own -- a life that is an example to others as how it is done.

The purpose of Life Masterpiece is to show you how to tap the power you were born with and how to tap into it every single day. And to make it an effortless process so that it becomes a lifestyle.

Before I go any further, I want to thank you for your friendship. Even though I have never met you, personally, I feel as if you and I are kindred spirits. The reason why say that is it you picked up this book. You made an investment. You're now reading it. This means you are one of the few who will do what others will not. This puts you light years ahead of 99% of the people. You and I encounter every day. Those people are living a paint-by-numbers life. They want to change, but they just do not get it, because they haven't got the first clue what they want and worse, they are not willing to do anything to change it.

I know you're special because you are researching and exploring and because you are reading this. It says something to me about you. It tells me that you are willing to do what it takes to succeed. It tells me that you are not satisfied with your life, and you will not be satisfied until you have successfully created your own masterpiece. So, I really want to give you the tools that can make a difference.

I have dedicated my life to understanding what makes people do what they do. What drives you? What is it that makes the difference in performance from one human being to the next? If we are all born with the same stuff, what causes some to tap into it and others to settle for a mediocre, paint-by-numbers existence?

Power comes from concentrating your focus and taking daily action to improve something. Even a 1% improvement today can result in unbelievable change, because 1% per day will not give you a 365% difference in being the year, because it builds and compounds to create a difference, way beyond anything you can probably imagine right now.

I will show you how to make it happen quickly, not 10 or 20 years from now, but today. Anything you commit to and focus on everyday must improve.

The challenge is that most of us do not know WHO we are, and therefore do not know how to control our mental focus. In fact, most of us focus on what is not working and spent most of her energy focusing on what we DON'T want by asking questions like, “how come this always happens to me?” If you focus on that enough, then that is what you will continue to experience. (Universal laws don't work unless you reprogram).

I am going to show you how to refocus your mental energy and reprogram your subconscious, so that you can ask better questions and therefore get a better result. Whatever you focus on, you manifest, which is why the Law of attraction won't work until you know what you want at the deepest level of your mind.

The key is to get you to live by those factors. Most people focus on the small stuff. I know you are to believe this, or you would not have picked up this book. Most people are so focused on what they have to DO. In other words, they focus on their to-do list, how to make a living instead of how to create their life. You could so easily get caught up in the day-to-day experiences that you tend to make a monument of the port in your mind, when actually in the long term these things that seem monumentally important now are actually quite trivial.

To create your masterpiece, you have to learn how to take care of the big things -- each color in your crayon box -- mentally, emotionally, physically, financially, and spiritually. Here are two things that usually lead to ultimate success -- either inspiration or desperation. Desperation can be a good thing because until you get really dissatisfied. You won't do anything to take your life to another level. Dissatisfaction is awesome! If you are completely satisfied, you will get comfortable. They may life begins to deteriorate.

My guess is that you invested in this book because on some level you are dissatisfied.

("If you make enough money, at least you can handle your problems in style" R)

(Lots of money, beyond comfort zone)

"It's a funny thing, the more I practice the luckier I get" AP

Subconsciously, most of us have an idea of what we think we deserve. This is our comfort zone, in which the subconscious mind determines when it sets our internal thermostat. Your subconscious mind has set your internal thermostat, and so when you begin to achieve, perhaps make a lot of money, you begin to sabotage your success dropping down to where you subconsciously think you deserve to be.

The past does not equal the future. Even if you are jaded and cynical, you've tried everything, this moment is a great new opportunity if you've tried other programs in the past that nothing has really changed your lifelong term. I believe that all it has done is it has prepared you for this program. And at some level if you did not believe that, then you would not be reading this right now.

Life Masterpiece is very different from other programs you may have tried. You will not find affirmations and visualizations and motivations in this book. What you will find is the answer to what is keeping you back, and how to reprogram your subconscious mind and how to use it to create.

Your brain is the most powerful computer on the planet. When you learn to use it properly, you can create any result you want. And they can give you the answer to almost any problem you have. The problem is that this computer, we call our brain, is not user-friendly, and does not come with an owner's manual. Life Masterpiece will show you how to operate your supercomputer with precision. Lasting change is not created in your life by learning more. Lasting change is created by using your own power to take action.

We're going to recondition the way your mind works by reprogramming your subconscious. This will change the way you feel and the way you behave for the rest of your life. Just as there have been extraordinary technological, scientific, and medical breakthroughs in the past two decades there has also been a breakthrough in the science of quantum physics. While we are not going to learn specifically about quantum physics in this book, we are going to take and use part of that technology. Because the latest cutting-edge tools for creating lasting change come from breakthroughs in quantum physics that have to do with human technology and how to get new results in record time.

There are four steps to success:

- ✓ Know what you want. It is important for you to know what you want, and for you to know how you want things to turn out. In other words, you must know your outcome before you begin. The first step is to decide what you want out of whatever situation you are currently in. The clearer you aren't what you want, the more you will empower your brain to give you the answers.

- ✓ You must use it. In other words, you must get yourself to take action toward your outcome. This means that you must put energy in the right direction, even when you do not know exactly what to do. Many people do not know what to do first. I will teach you exactly what to do. Some people want to know what happens if they try, and it doesn't work. I can tell you right now, and you will learn why in this book, why nothing you try will ever work. So how do you take action? Decide to. It's not about what you can do. It's about what you will do.

- ✓ Notice your results. It's not enough to take action. You must also pay attention to the results you are getting from your actions. Do your actions always work? No. Remember, success is just a series of failures, but failures with the purpose, failures directed at a specific result. You know what you want; you took action, now notice the result. (JS-obstacles and timing).
- ✓ Be flexible and willing to change your approach. You must be willing to make changes and adjustments based on the results of your actions, because flexibility is the key to the system. In other words, if you notice that what you are doing is not working. And you're not getting closer to your goal or even getting further away, instead of feeling like a failure in giving up. Sometimes you simply need to change your approach.

There is a way to speed this up. Instead of just knowing what you want, taking random actions, I will show you a way to increase the pace and the certainty of your success.

("Knowledge is not power. Knowledge is potential power." R)

You may be thinking, "Jim, if this is a simple, how come everyone isn't doing it?" The answer is because the majority of people tend to get caught up in the day-to-day trivialities such as paying their bills. Now, paying your bills might seem monumentally important to you, but honestly, can you think of anyone who has ever reported that they were successful in life because they mastered the art of bill paying? I am not saying that you shouldn't pay your bills, what I'm saying is that you should know I yourself to get caught up in something trivial and make it something big, so that you can use it as an excuse for not doing the really important things in life. At the end of your life, no one is going to remember whether or not you paid all of your bills and what a wonderful job you did of it. In other words, people get caught up in making a living instead of creating a life. They come to the end of their life dissatisfied because they realize they only live 10% of it, not because they were not capable or intelligent, and not for a lack of knowledge, but simply because they never had a clear idea about what they wanted.

Some people think that what they really want is a program that deals with only one area of your life like that business program. If that is what you are thinking, let me tell you right now that Life Masterpiece is one of the most powerful business programs because it deals with the source of all your business -- YOU. When you are better will be a better speaker, salesperson negotiator. Your creativity will flow freely. Mobile to manage and influence people far more effectively than you can now. The first step to changing your career and your business is to change yourself.

***

To contact Jim:

www.lutesinternational.com

info@lutesinternational.com

https://www.facebook.com/jimlutes

https://mindmotionacademy.com

Angie Carlson

With 20+ years in the finance sector, I bring experience, boldness, and compassion to the world of personal finance. My ten years as a financial aid director, combined with my education in mathematics and communications, give me the unique qualities needed to help my clients realize financial success in all areas of their lives. Carlson Financial Coaching was built through years of my own financial experiences and successes and the victories I celebrate alongside my clients. Whether you're looking to cut expenses, fund that next holiday vacation, save for that big-ticket item, or focus on finding your shared vision, I can help you create a plan and put it into motion. When not helping clients realize their financial dreams, I am curled up with my latest favorite book or spending time with my husband and two sons. The first conversation with me is always at no cost.

Nearly Losing My Life Showed Me How to Live the Life I Dreamed of

By Angie Carlson

The sterile room at the doctor's office seemed close in on my spouse and me as the surgeon delivered the news. "You have 50-50 odds of surviving the surgery," he said with unwavering eye contact. My husband and I exchanged a glance, then looked at each other in shock. At that moment, everything in my life shifted. The future became a precarious balance between hope and uncertainty.

The events leading up to this surgery started in the summer of 2017. I was attending a financial aid leadership event focused on the future plans of the state organization. Overnight, my body decided to override my brain. Waves of nausea hit—vomiting 20 times in an hour. Then, it would stop as fast as it came on. I was able to eat and drink like nothing had happened. Pregnancy was ruled out. When I got home, a doctor's visit led to a diagnosis of cyclic vomiting syndrome. While inconvenient, it wasn't a big deal. I picked up my prescription and went back to living my life.

Early 2018 revealed another symptom: severe back pain, concentrated in the upper right quadrant. The pain was relentless; over-the-counter pain meds were useless. I went back to the doctor, only to receive a clean bill of health. The pain persisted to the point that it was interfering with my day-to-day life. Desperation led us to the emergency room, where blood tests showed nothing amiss. "It must be in your head," they said. Frustration mounted as we returned home, my condition deteriorating.

Weeks turned into months, and I was now visiting the emergency room frequently. The medication was no longer helping with the random vomiting. The pain in my back continued to increase. The emergency room staff told me the same thing each time: "Everything looks fine." Deep down, I knew I was not fine. There was something going on. I felt more helpless day-by-day. I was doing everything I could think of to get answers, just to be told there weren't any.

After a few months of this, physical therapy was presented as an option for my back. While I had no idea how that would help the vomiting, I was desperate for any additional pain relief. When physical therapy started, I did my exercises every single day. My back pain continued to worsen. My physical therapist would change up my exercises. That would provide relief for a day or two, just for the pain to return even worse. I was getting really scared because I just knew this wasn't normal.

At this point, it was all I could do to go to work. Each night I was so tired. I couldn't spend time with my spouse or two young kids – it was back to bed for me, just to wake up completely exhausted after eight-plus hours of sleep.

In 2019, my emergency room visits were more frequent, with new symptoms appearing regularly. My skin started to have a yellow tint that couldn't be hidden no matter how much makeup I applied. My eyes were hollow and dry. I had severe chest pain that would not stop. My workplace had a lot of stairs, and I was completely winded after walking up five of them as a 39-year-old woman.

My symptoms started to become apparent to my co-workers in the summer of 2019. I worked at a cosmetology school in the financial aid office, and the esthetics instructors were concerned about my skin. My office co-workers sometimes noticed my hands were two completely different shades. While I felt validated that none of these symptoms were in my head, I knew I needed answers – and I didn't want to keep seeking medical help just to be turned away.

A new symptom appeared on Labor Day 2019. I was visiting my parents with the kids and could not keep anything down – including water. After a full day of this happening, my dad took me to an emergency room in their area that took my insurance. Their staff listened to my concerns and gave me an IV with strict instructions for the medical staff in my town to follow up with some tests – and an ultrasound. I was so weak I couldn't drive the boys and me 90 miles to my home – which amplified the concern my parents had.

My primary care (nurse practitioner) was out of the office until Wednesday – her staff was able to work me in. The only food or drink I'd had since Saturday was the IV from the emergency room. Nothing else would stay down. Even wetting my lips resulted in vomiting. We all were praying the ultrasound had answers.

The technician reacted as soon as my image came up. Part of my was relieved - her reaction meant we had answers. Part of me was horrified – because whatever was going on had to be really bad for the technician to react that way. We were given strict instructions to stay in the area. Less than ten minutes later, we had an appointment with surgery. And that's when we got the life-changing news - without surgery, there was a 100% chance I would die. With surgery, my odds improved to 50/50.

What was my body trying to tell me for over two years? That I needed my gallbladder out. It had died in my body about two years ago (when all the symptoms started). I was now septic. My organs were on the verge of starting the shutdown process. Plus, the surgery had to be delayed because I was so dehydrated that immediate surgery would have killed me as well. I received a wheelchair ride to the hospital across the street for immediate admission.

The period between the hospital admission and surgery is one I'll never forget. After not being able to eat or drink for days, I was incredibly hungry and thirsty. The weather outside was incredible, and I didn't care. If my time had come to pass at 39, I was ready to go even though I wanted to see my kids grow up and my marriage continue.

With no energy to do anything else, I was left with my mind. My mind was replaying all of the regrets I had in my life. There are times I wish I would have made a different choice or trusted someone else. The regrets that I had. The one regret was a constant – that I was too chicken to go for my vision of helping others with their finances.

My entire career had been spent in the financial field – backend retirement processing, a tax season, and I was a director of financial assistance at the time. All of these were helping people… right? Why was this regret so front and center? Why was I so scared to leave this world without helping others do what they needed to do?

Lying in bed staring out the window, it came to me. My husband and I started our financial journey in late 2017 and were debt-free except for our mortgage in April 2018. Being debt-free changed our marriage in ways that I never thought were possible. The mental gymnastics of juggling payments stopped. We kept trying to seek out solutions for what was going on with me because we eliminated money as the main driver for our decisions. That is what I wanted to help others do. I told myself if I survived the surgery, I was going to figure it out.

As I was being put under for the surgery, I took a few moments to appreciate the life I had lived in case I didn't survive. I wasn't scared of death – I was elated to be out of the pain. When I woke up from surgery, my pain had lessened so much that I thought the white room I was in was a trip to heaven instead of recovery.

The surgeon was able to share why I had every symptom I experienced. For the first time on my two-year journey, I was confident that we had finally solved the correct problem. I was confident that my life would slowly start getting back to normal. I was terrified of keeping my word to myself – because I suspected that what I wanted to be was a financial coach, and I had no idea how to go about it. Is there a certification? How do I find clients? Can I really do that job?

It turns out that these were only the start of the questions I had on my journey to becoming a financial coach. My brush with death made it extremely clear how I wanted to coach. My focus would be on the financial equivalent of gallbladder removal instead of how to treat the vomiting, back pain, and discolored skin.

Prior to starting our financial journey (again) in 2017, my husband and I spent almost a decade doing a budget without making any financial progress. We felt stuck – no matter what we tried to do to get ahead, we would only see how we were getting further behind. From the restart of our financial journey in 2017 and going through my near-death experience (and more!) without taking on additional debt – we knew our financial situation had fundamentally changed. What were we doing that was the same? What we were doing that was different?

With every step we took, the process became clearer. We had a renewed sense of teamwork. We focused on what we wanted our future to look like instead of the life we were currently living. We were tired of working opposite shifts – I was Monday through Friday, sometimes Saturday days, and he was Friday – Tuesday nights – and only saw each other in passing. Our family time was non-existent. While these decisions saved us a lot of money – what cost had we paid for the savings? How much time have we already wasted that we can never get back?

That's when we started to talk about the vision for our relationship. What we wanted it to look like, where we were going, etc. We talked a lot about the reasons we wanted to achieve it, the memories we wanted to create with our kids while they were still home, and the legacy we wanted to leave.

One decision we both knew was required – changing our jobs. I gave a 16-month notice at my job to pursue the vision of becoming a financial coach. We knew that my spouse working nights was not ideal, so he started to look for a job that he loved, and that fit our lifestyle. He left the evening job in August 2021 – just to be let go from the new job that was all days less than forty-five days later. I accepted a new position that started the following week – and day hours – with the same result.

After two months of unemployment, he started a temporary job in January 2022. One that he was still working when my last day, April 28, 2022, came. I left my secure full-time job without knowing when we'd have health insurance again. Or any idea of what our future looked like. On May 2, 2022, my husband was offered a full-time position as a temporary worker, and he was accepted to start on May 8, 2022.

More than two years after stepping into the vision, it was finally starting to unfold. We got our family time back. Conversations were not something we had to do – they were something we wanted to do. The conversations weren't limited to our marriage either. Conversations were important to prospecting. Clients were saying yes to our work together and experiencing amazing results. The pieces were starting to fall into place.

As I stepped into my business – Carlson Financial Coaching – full time, it became crystal clear that three things were going to be required. First, helping my clients solve the true financial problem by digging deeper than what the symptoms were telling us, and second, having a way to test and experiment to see what would give us the best and fastest results, no matter what other financial experts say. And third, the focus was going to be on couples and money conversations because of the incredible impact I had experienced.

Things began to unfold. I hired coaches who accelerated my progress in ways I never dreamed of. I focused on conversations and networking, which led to me meeting some of the most incredible people on the planet. I learned that strangers on the internet can be your biggest fans and wildest cheerleaders.

It didn't come without challenges, though. I had to make some intentional decisions to walk away from people who are absolutely amazing because our paths just grew apart. The inner work – deep fears and concerns I thought I had addressed years ago – kept resurfacing in different ways. I often questioned if I was really cut out to do this work. Can I handle the level of rejection that is required as an entrepreneur?

I decided I could and leaned into the work. Now, I'm considered by many to be the money communication expert in the Midwest. My signature method – Agree & Achieve – simplifies money communication for couples because it starts with agreement. What do you know to be true? An agreement that can be as simple as we hate talking about money. We're tired of making six figures and being broke or being in shock that you two have accomplished your wildest financial dreams, have no clue what is next, and have no one to ask.

The Agree & Achieve method turns that agreement into your shared relationship vision. With my clients, we discussed up to three priorities because we value quick, sustainable transformation. At this point, we look at the numbers—because the numbers will transform to follow your shared vision when you two know where you're going. That's how the financial plan can happen no matter what curveballs life throws your way.

Any couple that is willing to come together has what it takes to talk about their money. The challenge is – you know your point of view. It's now what words to use so your spouse understands what you're thinking – and vice versa. Knowing what you two mean when you say common money phrases.

Things get really fun at this point. My clients experience a relationship with less stress while hitting their next life milestone with East. The stress now is that they have more money and can start to take back their time, which requires being able to vet a team to ensure your long-term needs and legacy are happening. No couple wants to do this work just to have more money in the bank.

I'm so blessed to be the one called into this work. While I have no desire to have another near-death experience until it's my time to go, I am so thankful that it happened. The wake-up call I needed turned out not to be for just me. It may be exactly what you need to see: your future is bigger and bolder than anything you can see.

After all, none of us are promised tomorrow. Have that hard money conversation with your spouse. Decide what you two want your relationship to look like. Go for it. Please don't wait until it's too late, and all you're left with is regrets about what could have been.

***

To contact Angie:

If you'd like to learn more about how I serve couples, download my free e-book Beyond the

Budget: 10 Money Principles to Accelerate Your Path to Reach Your Shared Financial Goals as a Couple here:

Beyond the Budget (carlsonfinancialcoaching.com)

Websites:

Carlson Financial Coaching, LLC

Carlson Financial Coaching (ramseycoach.com)

Email:

angie@carlsonfinancialcoaching.com

carlsonfinancialcoaching2@gmail.com

B. Von Squires

B. Von Squires is an inspirational author, mindfulness coach, and podcast host dedicated to helping others heal from even the deepest wounds. After experiencing psychological abuse and emotional neglect as a child and trauma issues throughout life, in her late 30s, B. set out on a profound journey of self-discovery and personal transformation.

Through intensive counseling, forgiveness, and cultivating a daily gratitude routine, B. was able to transform her past hardships into the motivation for her life's purpose—helping others do the same. She completed an MBA with a focus on healthcare. Trauma and recovery are her passions.

As a Life Coach, B. has supported thousands seeking renewal on their healing paths. Her warm, insightful podcast "The Healing Train" explores all aspects of trauma, resilience, and living an abundant, meaningful life after facing darkness. She also created the Emotional Healing Challenge, combining evidence-based therapeutic techniques with mindfulness, journaling, and community building.

B. Von's down-to-earth, uplifting style resonates deeply. She knows firsthand that even after unimaginable loss or pain, we each hold a light within that no circumstance can dim - we just need the right tools and support to let it shine through once more. For B. Von, this work is a blessing, a reminder of how far we can go when we refuse to give up on ourselves and each other.

A Journey of Self-Discovery and Healing

By B. Von Squires

I spent the last 20 years of my life healing. WOW! Let that sink in... day in and day out, for 20 years to heal the brokenness. That's a long time and a lot of mistakes. I finally got it right, but not before I hit the bottom.

I wandered in the relentless wilderness of life, repeating self-defeating trauma behaviors that eventually became ugly, stinky habits. I developed a pattern of living that led to self-loathing and a minimal desire for living. My social skills were reduced, and my vocabulary was depleted. One day, I looked into the mirror and was horrified at the monster I had become!

The guilt and shame of being me had finally beaten me down. Reliving the horrors of the past was too much. Like a drained battery, I had no life energy. I was ready to let go. I wanted to give up. The pain of psychological abuse and emotional neglect had become so ingrained that it led to the use of alcohol or drugs to escape the suffering. Suicide attempts became an option to escape the spiritual suffering and mental anguish altogether.

Most times, I only went out at night. It became a way of life to roam the streets all night. One night, I revisited this party house from the week before, looking for a safe place to sleep. When I arrived, the house was dark and empty, much like my soul at this point. I checked the front door, and it was locked. I went around back and gained entry through the open door. I called out, and no one answered. I think it was a full moon that night because I was able to see my way around much better than one would imagine. I could see that I was alone. I went to lock the back door and found a wooden board to push under the doorknob for safety.

I returned to the room where I had noticed the bare, dirty mattress earlier and pulled it to the front room; the smell was awful. I positioned the mattress so that I could see both the front and back doors. I began to cry; I mean sobbing at the state of my life. I asked myself, "How the hell did you get here?" I laid on that smelly, dirty mattress and cried out to God. "God, please, don't let this be my life.

Please God! Please, don't let this be my life." As I laid there in the filth, in the darkness, I attempted to trace my steps back to where my life had gotten off track. All I could feel was emptiness and abandonment as I realized I was unwanted, unseen, unheard, accepted, and unloved. As I imagined living more of the same hell that I had already been through, all I could do was cry and drink myself to sleep, hoping never to wake up. This was one of the darkest nights of my life, yet it was the night that I surrendered.

I understand trauma as a shock to your entire system that locks energy into the cells, muscles, organs, mind, emotions, and spirit. Imagine a car accident - when two automobiles collide, they are rearranged, and even after being restored to certified working condition, they will not be in their original state. If you are anything like me, you have suffered spiritual injuries in one form or another, whether direct or indirect; the consequences and the feelings of shame, guilt, anger, and remorse are the same.

My spiritual injuries took place so young in life that by the time I discovered the residual effects, it was too late; I had already become a product of my trauma. At the time of trauma, the emotional, mental, spiritual, and physical energy that was in play is thrust together and broken around each other in a baffling manner. The components are shocked together, inextricably tied and bound by the energy trapped within. That traumatic moment is forever frozen within the mind, body, and spirit of the injured soul, creating a mental loop that will negatively affect the emotional and physiological responses.

Unless the spiritual injury can be identified and treated, the special type of healing that is needed is never realized. Trauma becomes the lens from which life is endured and the blueprint for the mental programming on which living will be predicated. Spiritual injuries and our natural trauma response to them determine our beliefs and the agreements we make with ourselves. The pain of feeling such injuries drove me to create habits and behavior patterns to numb the feelings of inadequacy, depression, lack of motivation, and fear of never being successful in life.

After a rough day at the office or after being home all day with the children, you go to the kitchen, reach in the cabinet over the refrigerator, you know the one. You bring down the bag of cookies with the idea of eating one as you finish up the dishes. Before you know it, you look down, and more than half the first sleeve of cookies is "missing," yet you only remember eating the first one. Sure enough, tricking yourself into believing that a mouth full of brownies is just what you need to make you feel better. Even if, for a moment, the extra pounds are worth it. You tell yourself one more won't hurt, as you justify to yourself...anything not to feel the feelings.

I understand how trauma can distort our perspective. When we're wounded at a young age, it's so easy to internalize those painful "first times" and carry them into adulthood.

In my own journey of healing, I realized how many aspects of my life were shaped by attempts to regain control of emotions I'd suppressed as a girl. The obsessive need to fix past wrongs or repeat fleeting joys kept me stuck in unhealthy patterns for too long.

But healing doesn't have to be that way. It's all about reframing how we see ourselves and our experiences. Those "first times" don't define you - they were simply starting points on a lifelong path of self-discovery.

At some point, my total personality was developed around the trauma - thoughts, desires, and behavior are all part of a defective mental program. The thoughts, emotions, and actions are all patterns that recreate the crime scene in some manner in an attempt to "right the wrong." From the auto-programming that happens in the mental background whispering reminders that you are not good enough, you will not amount to anything, you don't matter, to the day-to-day activities that fill life. A broken, desperate child was hidden away inside, begging to be healed.

So, I went on as best I could, haunted by the memory of the spiritual wounds I was too young to understand, wounds my tiny body was too young to endure. My tiny spirit was broken and hurt through neglect and emotional, psychological, and physical abuse. My fragile personality was fractured by negative words of rejection, often by a parent I trusted and loved most. Will I ever feel loved?

Based on my limited understanding and inability to appropriately navigate the damaging thoughts and feelings, I created a psychological and emotional mask. I erected invisible walls to protect myself from being criticized. I developed strange mannerisms to hide my guilt and shame from others and eventually from myself. Based on these feelings and actions, I developed a world that kept me numb and dark. I would see glimpses of reality, but it was too painful to feel. I couldn't stand to be me.

We do the best we can to endure the effects of the spiritual injury; however, some go on to create a life of material wealth, yet one of spiritual and emotional bankruptcy. Often, things may look amazing on paper; you graduated top of the class; you speak multiple languages and are so much fun to be around. You have a career and family. You are the epitome of living itself. However, at the end of the night, after all the makeup is off, the music has stopped, the lights are off, and you are alone. What comes to mind? Are you satisfied with your life? Do you ever feel like you have everything and still have nothing? Do you feel that... That feeling sitting in the pit of your stomach as you replay the events of your life, doing your best to identify the instant when you became unhappy, and sadly, you can't remember a time when you truly were happy. You feel sad, like a complete failure, and voices in your head agree.

You can't seem to feel complete no matter how much power, property, or prestige you earn. Years go by, and you suffer in silence, thinking you are sure to be rejected if "they" only knew how incomplete you really feel. So, you call the doctor for a new prescription of "zanies" and tell yourself, "Well, I could be worse." Can you relate?

I have not found any way to separate my thoughts, feelings, and behavior into individual moments that do not influence each other. In my experience, feelings cannot be compartmentalized, and we cannot pick and choose how we will be affected by them. At some point, I grew to live with character flaws and learned to make excuses for them as if I were protecting my children. Trauma responses were intertwined with my thoughts, emotions, feelings, and desires.

Trauma created a representative of me, and all of my relationships were with this false persona.

I intentionally shaped and cultivated relationships to the extent that I adjusted my objectives to get what I wanted no matter the cost, I wanted instant gratification!! I fundamentally altered my essence, my very identity – and these alterations developed into destructive living patterns that led to unemployability, jail, overdose, sexual trauma, and unhealthy relationships.

My friends, I understand the darkness you've experienced. When life overwhelms us with challenges, it's easy to feel trapped in self-doubt, uncertain if we'll ever achieve inner peace or manifest our dreams. But I'm here to tell you - you have so much greatness within you, just waiting to unfold.

I know that place of spiritual darkness all too well—that heavy fog of depression and anxiety where your inner light seems dimmed beyond repair. But here's a little secret—our souls were never meant for darkness. We each hold a divine spark that no circumstance can extinguish. Even in our lowest moments, that inner flame still flickers, just waiting for us to give it breath again.

Rebuilding after trauma isn't easy. It requires courage, patience, and compassion for yourself - especially on those days when the shadows still feel all-consuming. But with each step you take toward healing, those shadows will lift bit by bit.

Progress isn't a straight line. There will be good days and bad. But keeping your eyes on the horizon of who you're becoming and having faith that light still exists—that's how renewal happens. Focus first on self-care and listening to what nourishes your soul each day. The rest will follow.

This process may feel long, but stay determined and keep showing up for yourselves with love. One sunrise at a time, your light will rekindle. Soon, you'll wake to find yourselves even brighter than before.

Making the decision to initiate change was a pivotal step towards reclaiming my inner peace and well-being.

I had to look inward at my emotional sadness, my emptiness. I had to give myself permission to reflect, cry, and recognize what was causing my pain. I was disturbed to realize that at this point, as an adult, I was causing my own pain. It was difficult to admit that, over time, I had allowed spiritual injuries to control every thought, feeling, behavior, and action. I came across a video on YouTube of Les Brown telling me that I had greatness running through my veins. I became motivated to take the first step towards building a solid foundation that will heal my spiritual wounds and restore my relationships with myself and others.

Broken and tired of living at the mercy of life, I needed a healing process that could bring me back to the scene of the crime – the root of the spiritual injury where empathy, support, love, and compassion provide the foundation for my healing. The Spiritual concepts of honesty, acceptance, surrender, open-mindedness, humility, trust, and willingness are the brick and mortar that became my foundation to practice healing my spiritual wounds and rebuild a truly meaningful and fulfilled life.

I was filled with hope as the days went by. I have a desire to build something of myself. I started a movement called Willingness Wednesday with the idea that I am willing to do the work to take my life to the next level. I began researching thought leaders and applying mental and spiritual concepts. I came to understand, as Don Miguel Ruiz states, that I was born into the dream of the planet. I have to become awakened to my reality. As I continued to research and study Deepak Chopra and other spiritual teachers, I learned about the multidimensional makeup of myself as a being. I came to understand trauma and how it affects our mind, body, and soul. I became willing to accept my responsibility to heal my life.

Healing takes courage, yet moving toward peace is its own reward. One step at a time, with compassion for myself, shadows lift—I've seen this truth in others and myself. Progress isn't a straight line; there will be good and bad. By keeping my gaze inward, I see who I'm becoming, believing that healing exists. Through prayer, meditation, visualization and imagination from the teachings of Dr. Silva, I was guided to co-create the most beautiful living I could can imagine!

Through positive thoughts, feelings, and actions, I have reached a new level of self-acceptance, which allows me to freely interact with God (Spirit), myself, and others without fear of rejection. I am amazed and filled with gratitude as I cultivate a level of self-love, I never knew was possible. I have come to know courage as I move forward in life with the skill to make decisions that lead to my total happiness.

I have found that physical and psychological therapies can address many parts of trauma, but without a spiritual component, healing is surface-level at best. Learning to connect my spiritual self with my physical and mental self through spiritual practice is a lifelong skill that adheres to the values and principles promoting happiness.

If you have the desire for living a life that is more fulfilling than you can imagine, if you are willing to do whatever it takes to recover your happiness and regain the inner courage to live authentically then you are ready to begin a powerful, enlightening journey through The Energy Harvest: A Spiritual Model for the Enhancement of Life, a four-phase systematic process of practical, intuitive, and spiritual healing experiences.

A structured healing process is best for tracking progress. I have outlined my process here.

In the **Identify Healing Phase**: Identifying trauma is a crucial step towards achieving a fulfilling and balanced life. Recognizing trauma and spiritual injuries in the context of energy harvesting has positively impacted my life.

Recognizing past traumas and spiritual wounds is the first step toward healing and moving forward. By acknowledging these experiences, I began the process of self-discovery and inner transformation.

Understanding the impact of trauma and spiritual injuries fosters self-awareness and introspection. It allows you to gain insights into your emotions, behaviors, and thought patterns, leading to impactful growth and development.

In the **Set Healing Phase**: a profound emphasis is placed on the significance of cultivating a forgiveness mindset. We dive into the importance of forgiveness in enhancing your life. The spiritual model revolves around the concept of energy harvest, where the energy we emit into the universe directly impacts the quality of our lives. Negative emotions such as anger, resentment, and grudges create a toxic energy that hinders personal growth and fulfillment.

In the **Achieve Healing Phase**: the concept of healing through spiritual practices is explored to provide insights into the possible achievements you can attain.

Together, we delve into the transformative potential of spiritual healing and energy harvesting, focusing on the benefits and outcomes that you, who are passionate about living life to the fullest and healthiest.

In the **Sustain Healing Phase**: the concept of personal sustainability is a key element in empowering resilience. We dive into the importance of personal sustainability from a spiritual standpoint, focusing on how it can enhance your life and foster resilience in the face of challenges. Personal sustainability encompasses the ability to maintain a healthy balance in various aspects of life, including physical, emotional, mental, and spiritual well-being. It involves making conscious choices that not only benefit you but also contribute positively to the environment and society around you.

This journey of renewal is really about reclaiming yourself—who you are beneath it all, your divine essence. I have faith that you can get there. You've survived everything life has thrown at you so far, which means you are unstoppable. One day soon, you'll wake up and see that you're even happier and more whole than you ever imagined. For now, just keep showing up for yourself with compassion and doing the work. You've got this.

I am B. Von Squires; I am blessed to have been given this divine vision and the power to move into action. I am an example of the impact that God's grace and mercy can have on your life. I believe my purpose is to educate, empower, and celebrate individuals on their trauma-healing journey. I am grateful for the small role that I play as your trauma-healing champion.

***

Contact Us:

Website: www.spiritsourceconnection.com

Email: spiritsourceinfo@gmail.com

Facebook: https://www.facebook.com/SpiritSourcecoaching/

Crystal Robinson

Crystal is a devoted mother of two, a loving wife, and a passionate advocate for health and wellness. As a National Board-Certified Health and Wellness Coach (NBC-HWC) and a Chopra Certified Total Well-being Coach, she combines her expertise as a Whole Health Holistic Nutrition Practitioner, Intuitive Energy Healer, Psychic, and Spirit Medium.

With over 30 years in engineering, including 17 as Vice President, Crystal brings a unique blend of analytical skills and compassionate service to her coaching practice. Her personal experiences with grief, anxiety, and chronic health challenges led her to understand the profound connection between mind, body, and spirit, integrating Eastern healing practices with Western medicine.

Crystal's mission is to help others uncover their inner strength and take charge of their health. She specializes in various practices, including Reiki, Quantum Healing, meditation, and holistic nutrition. Rooted in Vedic philosophy and evidence-based psychology, her coaching honors clients as the experts of their own lives, fostering autonomy, creativity, resourcefulness, and self-efficacy.

Through transformative coaching, Crystal guides individuals in cultivating awareness and understanding human behavior, facilitating profound breakthroughs. Her holistic approach encompasses mindfulness, Ayurveda, neuroscience, and positive psychology, providing a full spectrum of support to facilitate deep healing and purpose discovery.

Ultimately, she is dedicated to helping others live happier, healthier, and more fulfilled lives, illuminating their paths to wellness and purpose.

The Catalysts

By Crystal Robinson

Catalyst, noun (cat·a·lyst): an agent that provokes or speeds significant change or action.

I have this picture a friend gave me hanging in my home office. It's a drawing of a woman surrounded by colorful dragonflies. The caption reads, "I love the woman I've become because I fought to become her." So many quotes can be the summaries of our story; this one is mine.

I am an example of "The Body Keeps the Score." For over four decades, my childhood and adult traumas were pushed aside, down, and buried. I let them fester and become me. Yet I kept fighting regardless of the circumstances in my life. On one side, I was living in an awful place of victim mentality; on the other, I was, *"Pull up your bootstraps and trudge on." "Don't process the shame or guilt." "Don't show pain, weakness, or regret." "Keep the peace." "I can fix it." "I'll show them I can."* and *"No one can say I can't."* It was a crazy mental circle rooted in my nervous system from a stressful childhood. I was living in fight or flight, 24/7. My fight was behind the scenes. When it appeared on stage, my body was the instrument. The concept that disease in the body is due to **dis-ease**, more commonly known as **stress,** had manifested in me. Our brains will tell us many things to feel "safe." Mine was living in the comfort of chaos. The Brain is a wonderful, amazing, beautiful, awful, horrible thing.

My journey was fraught with mountains and ravines that I navigated with the energy of a naive fool. Similar to the Fool in tarot, always seeing the positive and jumping into anything with both feet, eyes closed. A rebel at heart and too curious for my own good, I was half tomboy, half "girly" girl. I built go-carts with my dad growing up, but I loved to dress up and wear makeup, too. I wanted to attend a technical high school for cosmetology. My dad had other intentions. My science and math scores were outstanding; I was allowed to pick between electronics and engineering. I graduated at the top of my class with numerous awards in the mechanical regimen. I really enjoyed figuring out how things worked and making them better. I started my engineering career in a co-op program. I went to night school for Cosmetology while working in engineering by day. Mostly to thwart my dad for telling me I couldn't and prove that I could.

My health concerns started in my teens. I got Migraine headaches till I vomited and go into a dark room to sleep. At thirteen, a large lump formed in my neck, under my jaw. The local doctor said it was cysts, and they were removed. They found swollen lymph nodes. We never knew the cause. My body was trying to tell me something, and I didn't know how to listen.

One night when I slept over at a friend's house, I was raped by her stepbrother. I was fourteen, and I never told anyone. I was embarrassed and ashamed. I blamed myself. I shoved it away and buried it in my mind. The following summer, I met my husband. We were both in the engineering program. He became the one constant, stable person in my life when I needed it the most. He is still my rock 36 years later.

In my early twenties, I was diagnosed with arthritis. Who gets that in their twenties? My fingers on both hands would ache so badly I couldn't use my hands without pain on many occasions. I was a mechanical engineer by day and a nail technician by night. My livelihood required my hands to be mobile and in precise control. The doctors would sometimes blame the pain on hypermobility or double joints. I would get a massively swollen wrist or ankle out of nowhere. No sprain or injury had occurred. Doctors would say I must have done something, put me in a splint, and tell me to rest. No actual cause was investigated. I felt like I was crazy or a hypochondriac. I didn't understand that the medical system was designed to treat symptoms and not find the cause. I would wonder why my digestion was so bad, and I lived with constant cramps, bloating, and bouts of diarrhea or constipation. But I was too embarrassed to ever talk to a doctor. This was Celiac Disease exhibiting in me. My body was now yelling at me to pay attention, but I was deaf to its outcries.

I started to work hard to take care of my body by going to the gym and following a healthy diet. I had struggled with my weight up and down throughout my twenties, two pregnancies, and into my thirties. I wanted to get back to being healthy, have more energy, and enjoy being with my young children. I ate Pistachio ice cream, and my lips and mouth went numb. I was nauseous. I took Benadryl. The same thing happened on a few other occasions. I was concerned but not alarmed. I didn't have allergies.

September 11th, 2006, I was making my three-year-old son a peanut butter and jelly sandwich. I got peanut butter on my finger and licked it off. After a few minutes, I felt this immense sense of doom wash over me. My lips and tongue went tingly, and I was very nauseous. I put my son down for his nap and called the doctor's office to talk to a nurse. She asked me if I had an Epi-pen. I didn't know what that was. She told me to call 911. After a long afternoon in the ER, it was determined that at thirty-three, I was severely allergic to peanuts and tree nuts. My body was now screaming at me, and I was scared. This was my first **Catalyst**, and it changed my life. The thing about a Catalyst is we don't expect things to get worse before they get better.

Through my thirties, I did everything I could to live the "normal" life I had been living before the allergies. My family took it all in stride for the most part. I was so afraid to eat anything that I lost 65 pounds in just over three months. I called it the fear diet. Unfortunately, allergies in restaurants didn't have a protocol back then, and I visited the ER many times. The mental toll was agonizing for both me and my family. In one year, I had anaphylaxis reactions six times. We learned during that time that I was also allergic to Soy.

Labor Day in 2013 became another defining moment for me. I consumed a leftover cupcake that I had made for a party we attended the day before. Since I had made them myself, I thought they were fine. I didn't realize how easily cross-contamination happens at a party full of children and food. I had an anaphylactic reaction in my own kitchen. I used my Epi-pen, called 911, and went to the ER again. This was the scariest reaction I had to date. The doctors were unsure about the medications, and my heart rate went crazy. I spent four days in the hospital, undergoing multiple heart tests. I was scared out of my mind that I was going to die and leave my two young children without their mother. When I was able to go home, I was outfitted with a heart monitor for a week. The stress of everything in my life and the medical traumas pulled me down into a hole of fear and despair.

I was afraid to eat and sometimes breathe. I was having anxiety and panic attacks constantly. I was so afraid that I was going to die that I was afraid to live. The doctors told me, don't eat nuts, you'll be fine. I was given medication just to breathe and go about life for my family. But that's exactly what it felt like. I was just there, not really living. I was eating only seven foods. I was so in my brain, living in fear. The medications could not solve that; they just made me numb. This took a toll on my work; my boss thought I was crazy and put me on leave. It also took a significant toll on my family. I am so grateful they were the foundation and walls that held me safe through the storm. A friend recommended a Holistic Nutritionist. I was willing to try anything. After 90 minutes with him and his EMT (Electromagnetic Muscle Testing). I had a food plan that I felt safe with. I was able to start living a better life, nourishing my body. That December, three days before Christmas, I was rushed to the hospital in the middle of the night in major pain. My gallbladder had become blocked and infected and was removed the next day. I was forty, and I was falling apart.

It was time for me to listen to my body. I started focusing on myself. I found a therapist who specializes in anxiety and medical trauma. I continued to work with the Holistic Nutritionist, adjusting my foods to what my energy and body needed. I started doing more things I enjoyed instead of only doing things for others. Going to yoga, making jewelry, and scrapbooking. That spring, I signed up for a Ballroom Dance Lesson. I knew I loved to dance. The first lesson was amazing. I jumped in with both feet. I signed up for competitions, shows, and all the things in between. I went to the studio at least two nights a week. It nourished my soul like nothing else. Within weeks, I was off the medications. This was my happy place. I was listening to not just my body, but my spirit.

Within sixteen years after graduating from technical high school, I became a Vice President of Engineering at a company that manufactures research and development tools for the top scientists and engineers around the world. I do not have an engineering degree. Although I remember my boss telling me to tell clients, I went to

Northeastern. I couldn't, and my integrity would not allow that. I proved my worth with my designs and didn't need a degree to show clients I was worthy. When I started there, in the mid-nineties, it was a small startup. I was the fourth employee; 28 years later, they have thousands of machines around the world in the most prestigious research labs and universities. I am extremely proud of my contribution there. I withstood many years of sexual harassment and bias as a woman in a male-dominated field. This took its toll on me. In 2017, when the Me-Too movement became an international phenomenon, I started to understand that what I was withstanding was not okay. I had thought that this was normal and required of me to succeed. This reared my victim mentality to a crescendo, but I was centered on my family's happiness, so I withstood. I had to hold up the bootstraps.

My commitment to dancing helped me get through the horrors in my brain working in that environment. I couldn't think about anything when I danced. It's a complete surrender for my brain. This helped my nervous system regulate itself. I lived in joy when I danced. I met wonderful people from different backgrounds and cultures who did amazing things. I created lifelong relationships I will have for the rest of my life. Dance is truly therapeutic for me. It was a **Catalyst** in the right direction. Unfortunately, that wasn't enough to heal. My body started alarming again.

This time, I was left dumbfounded. Pain in all my joints, especially my fingers, hands, and wrists. Swelling in both feet. Constricting pain in my rib cage, I couldn't be touched at times. I saw numerous doctors and rheumatologists. Rheumatoid Arthritis and Connective Tissue Disorder were mentioned as most likely causes. I was put on Steroids regularly and taking Advil like candy. I still danced some. I had to take breaks, sometimes weeks at a time. This illness would come and go like a virus, lasting weeks or months at a time. After my daughter's graduation, I got a sun rash called Lupus photosensitivity. *I had Lupus.* I was put on more medications, specifically for Lupus, and told this was not curable. I would have this for the rest of my life. Ummm, bootstraps, please?

It was so hard to pull them up this time. I gave in to the illness for a while. I stopped dancing and just tried to rest and take care of my body. Therapy, nutrition, exercise, yoga, journaling, meditation, dance, music, and my own intuitive energy work became priorities. I knew I had the power to heal and nourish this vessel. It needed to start with the connection of my mind, body, and spirit. I listened to amazing healers on podcasts and read any books I could get my hands on. Through it all, I learned that "Truth Leads to Healing". By the summer of 2019, I was living Lupus-free. I had done it. Then, the bomb dropped.

I performed in a show at the end of June. My balance didn't feel great. In mid-July, I accidentally whacked the back of my head on the corner of the TV. Hard enough to see stars. I got headaches, and my face started twitching strangely. I decided to get checked since we had a vacation planned. I didn't have a concussion; *I had a Brain Tumor*.

Golf ball-sized and behind my left eye. I needed anti-seizure medication and a surgeon. No vacation. This was a big **Catalyst**. I may not live through this. Brain surgery! Forget the bootstraps; I needed thigh-high stiletto boots! I was not giving up; it was time for research mode. I worked with the Brain Tumor Network. They found the best neurosurgeons in Boston. I had the amazing Dr. Chiocca, Chief of Neurosurgery at Brigham and Woman's Hospital. I spent the next week with my family before surgery. I made sure all the ducks were in a row. They were going to operate on my brain. They were opening up my skull. My family needed to be prepared. My husband wouldn't allow "what ifs." It was up to me to be the glue and keep it together. I could do this. I had Brain Surgery; the tumor was removed. A week later, we learned it was benign. I was going to be okay. I had some screws in my head now, but they were tight!

That changed everything. What was important and what mattered to me was completely rearranged. My mind, body, and spirit are more important than anything. I knew that if I was not taking care of myself, I couldn't take care of my family, my job, my life. I had nothing without my health. I no longer cared what other people thought. I understood in a profound way my purpose was to help others not get a brain tumor. Then, the Pandemic happened.

The world was turned upside-down. Strangely, a reset to the status quo. It changed everyone's outlook on life. Like a collective brain tumor, a shared **Catalyst**. We were all scared and horrified by what was going on in the world. But for me, after everything in my past, the fight or flight was my normal condition. I was oddly comfortable in chaos. That shouldn't be normal or comfortable. I continued my daily practices, especially meditation. I consumed more knowledge. I wanted to understand why my brain worked this way. During this time, I felt very alone. No one understood that the **Catalysts** had changed me.

I started seeing and hearing things from spirit. Am I crazy? Should I explore it, or shove it away? Very skeptical, I met with different mediums. I could tell strangers things about their loved ones. I knew what some people were feeling. The energy was palpable. I'm a medium. In September of 2021, my dad was in an accident. He endured massive brain trauma and was in an induced coma. He started talking to me in my head. His spirit was outside of his body, telling me what he wanted. It was strange and surreal. He didn't want to be there. He showed me the papers in my head. He kept saying, "The papers". By the time I found them days later, the doctors were pulling him out of the coma and he was seizing. The damage to his brain was too extensive. The papers, his living will, and health care proxy. He didn't want this, and I was his proxy. We made the decision to let him go. I felt the weight of him placing his hands on my shoulders; he said, "Thank you." That was the hardest thing I ever had to do. Harder than brain surgery. I will never forget that day. Before I went to say goodbye to my dad, my husband hugged me and said, "You're the strongest person I know." My dad is by my side every day. My spirit guides help when I'm befuddled and need to work through things in my crazy, beautiful, confusing brain.

Catalysts are a part of our lives. It's what makes us who we are and how we grow as individuals. Most are hard to endure, but we do endure. We get up; we trudge on. We pull up the bootstraps or get new boots. We grow from the catalysts. How long will you ignore the catalysts? What will you endure? Will you decide to listen, learn, and grow? The human mind, body, and spirit connection is as individual as our DNA. Your healing and growth journey is, too. Are you ready to decide to be happier, healthier, and more fulfilled? My Catalysts put me on this fulfilling path. Where will yours lead?

***

To contact Crystal:

For one-on-one coaching, group programs, workshops, or keynote speaking, please reach out to Crystal at Crystal Moon Holistic Healing.

Website: www.crystalmoonholistichealing.com

Email: crystallee@crystalmoonholistichealing.com

Facebook: www.facebook.com/crystalmoonholistichealing

Instagram: www.instagram.com/crystalmoonholistichealing

Daniel Erbe

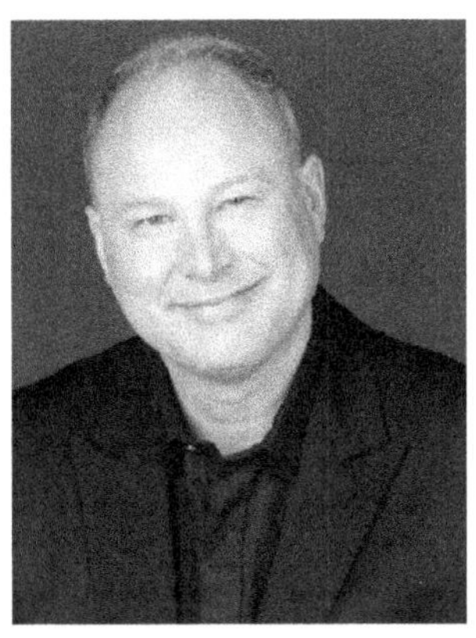

Award-winning singer Daniel Erbe is a resident of Virginia, a 13-year U.S. Army veteran, and an internationally acclaimed tenor who has performed for U.S. Presidents and global dignitaries. From 2009 to 2022, he served in the Grammy and Emmy-winning U.S. Army Field Band as a featured soloist, captivating audiences at high-profile events for the Military Joint Chiefs of Staff, celebrities, and the American public.

He has graced prestigious venues, including Carnegie Hall and the Kennedy Center, and has performed the National Anthem at major sports events like Fenway Park and Camden Yards. Daniel created the role of Jumper in the world premiere of ***The Falling and the Rising***, the first opera written for the U.S. Army, and is a featured soloist on the Grammy-winning album ***The Soundtrack of the American Soldier***.

As a Sergeant First Class, Daniel shared the Army story nationwide and continues to deliver patriotic music at various events, including twice at CPAC and for a global audience at the 2024 Republican National Convention. He has also established a voice and professional communicators studio, helping clients become influential, confident presenters. Daniel's expertise empowers them to elevate their performances and create genuine connections with their audiences, inspiring both on and off the stage.

"Discovering My Voice: Owning the Stage Through Trials and Victory"

By Daniel Erbe

I was drawn to peak performance from an early age, singing before I could talk. My mother, a musician, engaged me in musical games, and I have a recording of me singing "Happy Birthday" at two. My musical journey took off when I auditioned for the La Crosse Boy Choir at seven, impressing the director with my perfect recall. By nine, I was touring Europe with the elite "Ives Choir," at ten, I performed "Rejoice Greatly" from Handel's *Messiah* for thousands. Music was a deep-rooted part of my life, influenced by my mother, a bassoonist and educator, and my father, a professional tenor and military veteran. They instilled in me a passion for music and excellence, encouraging my exploration of various instruments and languages.

In second grade, I took my first acting role as Scrooge in *A Christmas Carol*, captivating the audience with my stage presence. In middle school, I joined the select choir, where I developed my singing and dancing techniques and picked up the trumpet. However, my family's relocation from Wisconsin to Kentucky at twelve forced me to leave friends behind and adapt to a new school, compounded by my parents' separation and eventual divorce. During this tumultuous time, music became my refuge.

High school provided a fresh start, where I grew physically and committed to peak performance while balancing competitive swimming. I earned fourth chair in the prestigious Lafayette High School Band, learning invaluable lessons about discipline and teamwork. As I transitioned into my adult voice, I became the youngest member of the Lexington Singers, performing alongside seasoned adults. My roles in *Fiddler on the Roof*, *South Pacific*, and *The Music Man* reinforced my belief that the stage was my sanctuary. Ultimately, I chose to focus entirely on music and theater, receiving accolades that fueled my passion.

Reflecting on high school, I see it as a whirlwind of growth and discovery, shaping my identity as a performer and leader and laying a strong foundation for future challenges and successes.

After receiving numerous scholarships, I chose to stay close to home and attend the University of Kentucky as a double music major in voice and trumpet performance, supported by full in-state tuition scholarships. I entered the program as the top freshman in the voice department, balancing a hectic schedule of marching band, singing in the opera, private lessons, academic courses, and fraternity life with Delta Sigma Phi.

Before my freshman year, I traveled with the Cavaliers Drum and Bugle Corps, earning a spot as fourth-chair upper lead soprano bugle and participating in the 1994 World Cup Parade and the Drum Corps World Championship.

A pivotal moment occurred during my freshman year when I discovered a video of Puccini's *Turandot* at the Arena di Verona. The powerful performances of tenor Nicola Martinucci and soprano Ghena Dimitrova inspired my desire to project my voice, igniting my passion for opera.

At the University of Kentucky, I focused on operatic training, vocal techniques, and stagecraft. My first operatic experience was in *The Magic Flute*. By junior year, I had participated in multiple opera scenes and was cast as "Little Bat" in *Susannah*, which taught me to separate my emotions from the character's.

At the end of my sophomore year, I underwent evaluations for performance majors. The faculty recognized my talent in singing and encouraged me to focus on it more, leading to multiple finalist awards from the National Association of Teachers of Singing (NATS). My voice teacher also urged me to explore my tenor range, igniting my ambition to master my technique like legendary tenors Pavarotti and Caruso, marking the beginning of a decade of dedicated work to develop my vocal technique, particularly for high notes.

Despite facing vocal challenges, my passion for singing remained strong. A masterclass with vocal pedagogue Shirley Emmons revealed my struggles with high notes, but my dedication and stage presence led to continued success in auditions. I took a year off between my bachelor's and master's degrees to solidify my transition from baritone to tenor before pursuing a master's in Vocal Performance at The University of Arizona.

In the summer of 2004, after returning to Kentucky from Tucson, I connected with renowned pedagogue Inci Bashar in Chicago. She helped me reconnect with my baritonal chest voice, rebuilding my vocal technique and making tenor roles more manageable. A significant moment came during a training program in Dierbach, Germany, where renowned soprano Jane Castleman encouraged me to pursue a career in Europe.

In the fall of 2005, I joined the Lyric Opera of Kansas City as a tenor apprentice, receiving a full tuition scholarship and stipend. My artistic director emphasized my musicality and stage presence, which was crucial as I developed a peak performance mindset, yet he was unimpressed by my voice. A memorable experience was preparing for *Carmen*, where my professionalism led to contracts for four roles that year. I networked with many working opera singers and began to feel like a professional.

I lived by the principle of being overly prepared, ensuring I was fully memorized before every rehearsal. This mindset, rooted in advice from my undergraduate years, emphasized that talent alone isn't enough; dedication to excellence leads to opportunities. In the summer of 2007, I performed in *La Vie Parisienne* at the Lake George Opera Studio where, according to the general director, my character stole the show, affirming my growth as a performer.

In 2008, after three years in Kansas City, I moved to Boston for two reasons: to be closer to New York for auditions and to reconnect with my father, whose support had been vital throughout my career. My parents' divorce had strained family ties, and this move allowed me to spend more time with my dad and stepmom, encouraged by my sister.

Unfortunately, this period also marked the onset of serious back pain from a previous production. Despite these challenges, I pursued my passion for opera, commuting 1.5 hours to work and performing at night. I participated in various productions in Boston, including an abridged *La Bohème* and a full production of *Carmen* as "Don José."

In the fall of 2008, a close friend encouraged me to audition for the Soldiers' Chorus of The United States Army Field Band (TUSAFB) despite my initial determination to focus on opera. After securing a new agent and performing in several Boston operas, I decided to audition for the Soldiers' Chorus, while my agent urged me to consider moving to Europe for more opera opportunities. Ultimately, I submitted my audition materials to the Army and was granted an in-person audition.

In the spring of 2009, I auditioned for the Army and was offered a spot in the Soldiers' Chorus. This was my most successful audition that year, leading to a tough decision: pursue my European opera dream, move to New York for auditions, or accept the Army position, which offered financial stability, including student loan repayment, a steady paycheck, and medical benefits. After discussing with my family, Inci, and my agent, I chose to accept the Army position, marking a turning point in my life.

In September 2009, I began basic training at Fort Benning, Georgia, facing significant challenges as a 32-year-old among younger recruits. The physical demands worsened my persistent back issues, and I relied on 1,200 mg of ibuprofen daily. Additionally, I developed lower-lobe pneumonia, leading to a week in the infirmary. After recovering, I qualified on my rifle and earned the sharpshooter badge, boosting my morale.

The final hurdle was the physical training test. After being sidelined for three weeks, I struggled with the physical effects of pneumonia but pushed through and passed my P.T. test. After basic training, I flew to Maryland to join TUSAFB, where I was promoted to Staff Sergeant just a month after graduation, an honor I never took for granted.

My first concert with the Soldiers' Chorus was in Spring 2010, where I performed solos of "America the Beautiful" and "Bridge Over Troubled Water." During our second tour stop in Youngstown, Ohio, I felt nervous but ready after a strong soundcheck. Performing on stage was exhilarating, and my leader's pride made me feel accomplished.

Following this tour, we prepared for the *PBS Memorial Day Concert* sharing the stage with Gary Sinise, Joe Mantegna, and Lionel

Richie, and found myself in the presence of the military Chiefs of Staff, some of the most influential people in the country-it was surreal. A pivotal moment came in July when I sang "America the Beautiful" with the Atlanta Symphony Orchestra in front of over 15,000 people, showcasing my ability to perform under pressure.

We also performed at Ford's Theatre for a July 4th event, where I had the honor of shaking hands with President Obama and Colin Powell. One of my first significant projects in TUSAFB involved producing an opera performance, culminating in a successful show at the Kennedy Center's Millennium Stage in February 2011.

During my time with the chorus, I performed nationwide, including the national anthem at iconic venues like Fenway Park, and as a soloist at Rupp Arena, where I sang for over 22,000 fans. After Hurricane Maria, the chorus participated in a healing mission to Puerto Rico and performed for millions at events like Boston's Fourth of July celebration. We also had the honor of singing at George H.W. Bush's funeral with the Armed Forces Chorus in front of five living presidents.

A memorable concert occurred in Delaware, where a 100-year-old World War II veteran stood to salute us during "God Bless the USA," highlighting the deep connection between music and patriotism.

In the spring of 2013, the Department of Defense was under sequestration, restricting travel for the Army Field Band. This prompted us to focus on local concerts to maintain our public connection. Our opera scenes concert series became a staple, allowing me to utilize my operatic training. After the successful production of the abridged *Così fan tutté* at the Kennedy Center, a colleague initiated an ongoing opera scenes program that contributed to *The Falling and the Rising*, a significant project for our organization.

These performances showcased operatic talents in local settings, supported by a professional director, pianist, and conductor. Additionally, I requested leave to travel to Germany to audition for opera agents and companies, marking an exciting new chapter in my journey.

Facing personal struggles, I questioned my role as a tenor in the Soldiers' Chorus, battling limiting beliefs and the fear of losing my operatic dream. After an unsuccessful audition tour in Germany, I returned home, reflecting on my experiences and seeking a new vocal technique.

After years of choir singing, I developed a constricted technique to blend into the tenor section, leading to muscle fatigue and deteriorating vocal health. By 2016, the toll of singing in distinct styles for choir and opera affected my confidence and performance, making me fear vocal failure and lose my vocal identity.

Recognizing the need for change, I sought new lessons, looking for new vocal tutelage. I eventually reconnected with Dr. Everett McCorvey, who referred me to voice specialist Dr. Joseph Stemple at the University of Kentucky. Through vocal function exercises, he discovered my vocal cords were overlapping due to excessive air pressure and improper adduction, a revelation that transformed my approach.

Under Dr. Stemple and Dr. Gregory Turay, I learned to approximate my vocal folds correctly, focusing on exercises that stabilized my larynx and reduced unnecessary pressure. This gradual healing restored my voice and confidence, proving that perseverance leads to renewal.

In 2017, I was chosen to create the role of "Jumper" in *The Falling and the Rising*, an opera about a Soldier's resilience after an IED explosion. My dedication and preparation led to recognition during my performance at Texas Christian University and at OPERA America's New Works Forum in New York City, allowing me to contribute my voice to a narrative that resonates deeply with my journey of overcoming challenges and embodying resilience.

I am proud to have recorded *The Soundtrack of the American Soldier* album at Skywalker Sound Studios, a significant project for the U.S. Army Field Band and Soldiers' Chorus. Collaborating with Grammy-winning audio engineers Leslie Ann Jones and Michael Romanowski and producer Dan Mercurio, the album features music from military-themed films, including *American Sniper*, and compositions by renowned composers like John Williams.

I was honored to be one of two featured soloists singing "Over There." Recording in the same studio where *Star Wars* was made felt surreal, and I knew my performance had to be exceptional since millions would hear it. This effort paid off when the album won a Grammy Award for Best Immersive Audio Album at the 63rd Grammy Awards.

This experience was a career highlight. It allowed me to showcase my expertise to the Hollywood music industry and reminded me of my passion for singing despite challenges.

During the 2020 pandemic, the Army Field Band transitioned from in-person concerts to online performances, resulting in over 320 videos that reached 103 million viewers and generated $34 million in earned media value. I played a key role in this shift, creating various online concerts, including a personal project honoring my family's military service.

The pandemic prompted deep reflection, leading me to seek a change in direction. As rumors of a COVID-19 vaccine mandate circulated, my unit took on emergency response roles, and I was tasked with documenting vaccinations. In response to the mandate, I requested medical and religious exemptions, believing God guided my decision. Despite presenting a compelling case, my exemptions were denied, and I faced pressure from leadership regarding my future in the Army.

At the Pray, Vote, Stand Conference in 2021, I met singer Mary Millben, whose patriotic songs stirred my emotions about singing. After sharing my story with her, she prayed with me. Little did I know I would share the stage with her at the RNC National Convention just a few years later.

Despite the pressure to conform and rumors of dishonorable discharge, I remained firm in my beliefs. For many reasons, including the mandate, a potential political career, and a solo singing career, I chose not to reenlist, believing it was the right decision. My final year was challenging, but I received an honorable discharge and full benefits, a fortunate outcome compared to many Soldiers in similar situations. Approximately 8,000 service members made this choice, each with their own reasons. My story is just one of many.

Reflecting on my experiences, I see how staying true to my convictions opened a new chapter, allowing me to pursue my values and advocate for those in need. The Army later rescinded the vaccine mandate, enabling some Soldiers to return, though few chose to do so.

Through sacrifices and challenges, I discovered purpose and reaffirmed my commitment to my beliefs. After my military career, I became politically active, joining the campaign trail in Georgia for Brian Kemp and Herschel Walker. During the 2022 Senate runoff, I traveled the state, recruiting canvassers and singing at events, including the College Football Hall of Fame rally, which rejuvenated my love for singing.

My singing career continued with an invitation to perform at the Conservative Political Action Conference (CPAC) for the Ronald Reagan Dinner, where I connected with influential figures and performed on international T.V., gaining recognition to veterans and as a soloist once more.

Focusing on my job as a communication specialist at the Pentagon and attending in-person ceremonies and events made me realize I could help others improve their public speaking. This idea intensified after I was released from a second government contract, prompting me to consider starting a coaching business. After consulting with a music business coach, I decided to help all types of communicators, not just singers.

In February 2024, I began my journey as a voice and communications coach, forming an LLC, building my brand, and networking to understand people's communication struggles. In spring 2024, I was invited back to CPAC D.C. to perform on the main stage, which allowed me to connect with notable figures, including J.D. Vance and Vivek Ramaswamy, and reinforced my passion for singing and public speaking. This experience solidified my vision to help others discover their authentic voice and command their stage, leading to the establishment of my coaching business.

The highlight of my three-decade singing career came when I was invited to sing the national anthem at the Republican National Convention (RNC). This opportunity felt like a defining moment, and I dedicated weeks to preparing vocally and mentally, fully committing myself to God, and visualizing my performance. The day before the event, I took a peaceful walk by Lake Michigan, listened to devotionals, and sang on the pier, centering myself on what was to come. On the performance day, I felt an incredible sense of peace and purpose. As I stepped onto the stage before roughly 25,000 people and a worldwide audience, I sang not just for the crowd but to give glory to God. My voice soared as I connected deeply with the moment, feeling grounded and focused. This was one of the largest audiences I had ever performed for as a soloist, and I truly felt I had arrived.

The performance was a success, met with a warm response from the audience. I saluted the crowd as a gesture of military respect, reaffirming my identity as a performer. My experiences at CPAC and the RNC solidified my vision of representing veterans on a worldwide stage and helping communicators unlock their voice of leadership and command their stage.

Writing this chapter in the Change Series book allows me to resonate with those who may have lost their voice, either literally or figuratively, or are searching for a way to command their stage. My journey illustrates that reclaiming one's identity and purpose is possible, even amid adversity.

Life has been full of challenges, often positioning me as the underdog. Yet, it all comes down to perseverance, preparation, determination, hard work, focus, and prayer. Since giving my life to Christ in my early twenties, He has been the driving force behind everything I do. I've tried to do things on my own and failed many times. Without Him, especially on stage performing for thousands, I would have nothing. I can't rely solely on myself without risking failure. God is the force behind all my efforts.

Now, I believe my purpose is to help others overcome obstacles, stage fright, performance anxiety, and vocal fatigue, guiding them to discover their authentic voice. It's about empowering people to discover their voice, command their stage and connect with their audience. While the media has now recognized me as a "Conservative Celebrity," I am excited to share my experiences with people from all walks of life.

This is the journey I am on now.

At the end of my RNC performance, I asked God, "Is this the end of my singing career?" He responded, "This is only the beginning."

As I write this, I will share the stage with Tucker Carlson, RFK Jr., Don Jr., Russell Brand, and other influencers at the Parallel Economy Public Square Summit in just a few weeks. It's a privilege to continue performing while using my experiences to inspire and uplift others.

***

To contact Daniel:

www.danielerbe.com

https://www.linkedin.com/in/danielerbeofficial/

https://www.facebook.com/danielerbe.official/

https://www.instagram.com/danielerbe_official/

The Commanding Voices Program

Daphne Paras

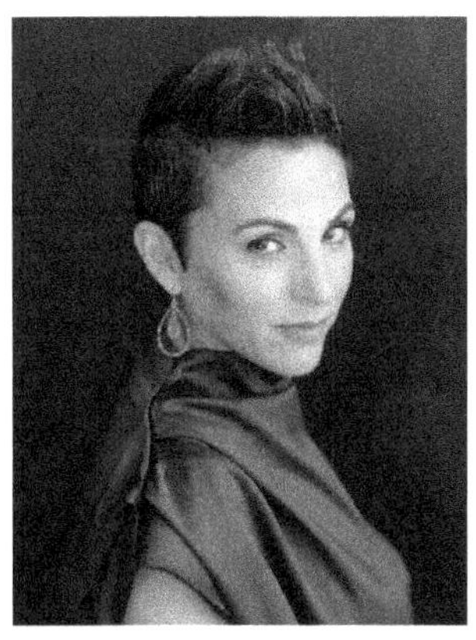

Daphne is a dynamic leader who ignites the fire within others and guides them toward profound transformation. With a passion for facilitating corporate and private programs, seminars, and workshops, she excels at creating safe, supportive spaces where participants can dive deep into the wisdom of their bodies—believing this is where true magic happens. Daphne leads by example, embodying the philosophy of being both teacher and student, always committed to learning and expanding her understanding of human potential.

Daphne's expertise spans empowerment, reclaiming one's voice, sacred sexuality, returning to the authentic self, Toltec spirituality, and public speaking/presenting. One of her most powerful tools for helping people become fully present in their bodies is firewalking, where participants learn how to raise their energy to cross 1800-degree coals. She also leads sacred journeys to the pyramids of Teotihuacan, Mexico, offering exclusive access to energetic epicenters never open to the public.

Her passion lies in helping women identify where trauma resides in the body and guiding them through pathways to clear and heal it. This journey inspired her to design and invent *The Seeker*, a sacred self-exploration and pleasure tool.

Her work is a testament to her mission: to inspire, heal, and empower others to embrace their fullest potential.

Sacred Sexuality: A Gateway to Your Authentic Self

By Daphne Paras

We often hear about the importance of being our "authentic self," especially in the realms of communication and connection. As a professional speaker and master facilitator, I've found that authenticity is one of the most powerful ways to truly connect with an audience. The same principle applies to any interpersonal exchange—authenticity fosters more profound, meaningful connections.

Yet so many of us don't truly know who our authentic selves are. We've buried parts of ourselves under layers of cultural norms, conditioning, and past experiences. I invite you to explore a different way of being, one that allows you to reveal and embrace your authentic self through the transformative power of Sacred Sexuality.

Authentic Self

The authentic self refers to a person's true, core identity, free from external influences, societal expectations, or pretenses. It's the version of oneself that is most genuine, reflecting one's deepest values, beliefs, feelings, and desires. Living as the authentic self involves aligning actions, choices, and behaviors with inner truths rather than conforming to what others expect or what may be imposed by social standards. It allows a person to live in congruence with their true self. Key attributes of the authentic self, include Self-awareness, Honesty, Vulnerability, and Alignment.

Sacred Sexuality

The most profound and effective path I have found back to our authentic selves, with deep healing and reconnection, is through our connection to our Sacred Sexuality. Sacred Sexuality is perhaps the most underutilized tool in our toolbox. For most, it lives in the shadows. Why?

When we experience trauma or pain, it is an uncomfortable feeling, and our innate response is to disconnect from it. This includes disconnecting from our sexuality, which can be short-term or for much longer periods of time. When disconnection occurs within our body, it cuts us off from our life force energy and strips away the very essence that fuels creativity, passion, and self-expression. This collective wound has carried through time, affecting not just individual experiences but also the collective consciousness of women.

Societal, cultural, familial, and historical forces have long dictated how we should view our sexuality, embedding themes of shame, guilt, and repression that begin in childhood and persist throughout our lives. One of the most significant barriers to accessing our Sacred Sexuality is the deep wounding we carry around our bodies, desires, and sexual expression.

From a young age, many women are exposed to messages that frame their bodies as either shameful or objects of control rather than as sacred vessels of pleasure and self-expression. These messages often begin in childhood, where concepts of modesty, purity, and "proper" femininity are instilled, creating a foundation of guilt, fear, and repression around sexual desires and bodily autonomy. Cultural and religious teachings have historically played a major role in this suppression. Women have been taught to prioritize the desires and comfort of others over their own sexual needs.

At a familial level, these forces are often passed down through generations. Mothers, aunts, or other female figures may unconsciously perpetuate cycles of shame by teaching young girls to suppress their sexuality or view it with suspicion and judgment. The unspoken rules around "appropriate" behavior, silence on topics like menstruation or sexual pleasure, and avoidance of discussions on healthy sexual exploration reinforce the idea that sexuality is something hidden, to be ashamed of or avoided.

Historically, women's bodies and sexual power have been controlled and repressed through various means, including laws, religious doctrines, and societal taboos. When women experience natural sexual desires or curiosity, this can lead to feelings of confusion and guilt. The weight of these societal, cultural, familial, and historical pressures often manifests in a disconnection from the body and a lack of understanding or appreciation for one's sexual desires and pleasure. The shame and guilt embedded in these experiences often prevent women from fully embracing their sexuality as a natural and sacred part of who they are. This disconnection from our Sacred Sexuality leads to feelings of inadequacy, low self-worth, and an inability to fully express themselves—whether in intimate relationships, creative pursuits, or in life in general.

Healing these wounds is essential to reclaiming our authentic selves but requires conscious effort. It involves unraveling the layers of conditioning that tell us our desires are "wrong," our bodies are flawed, and that pleasure is something to be hidden. Healing begins when we replace the narratives of shame with love, acceptance, and reverence for our bodies as sacred vessels of life, creativity, and pleasure.

One of the key aspects of Sacred Sexuality is cultivating emotional intimacy with oneself. Emotional intimacy means being willing to feel all of your emotions, no matter how uncomfortable or painful they may be. It means holding space for your own grief, anger, sadness, and joy. Through this process of emotional release, we begin to clear the blockages that prevent us from fully experiencing pleasure and connection.

The Feminine Experience of Sexuality

Sexuality is shaped by a woman's emotional, psychological, and spiritual connection to herself and her body. Our womb space, which applies whether or not you currently have a womb, is our epicenter of creativity. This is the place from which we literally create life. When we disconnect, we sever the flow to the core of our creativity. It is extremely challenging to be our full, authentic self when we are shut off from the flow of our creative life force energy.

For women, sexuality is experienced through a combination of physical, emotional, and psychological aspects. Key areas that play significant roles are reproductive organs, breasts, pelvic region, brain and nervous system, heart and emotions, and the body as a whole.

Reclaiming the Divine Feminine

In many spiritual traditions, sexuality is seen as a gateway to higher consciousness and deeper self-awareness. For women, reconnecting to our Sacred Sexuality often means reclaiming the feminine essence that has been suppressed or neglected. This essence is not just about sexual expression but about embracing the feminine qualities of intuition, receptivity, creativity, and emotional wisdom.

The Divine Feminine is cyclical, flowing, and deeply connected to nature and the rhythms of the earth. Our wombs mirror these cycles, reflecting the phases of creation, gestation, birth, and death. When we tap into this innate wisdom, we gain access to a profound source of power and creativity that flows through our bodies.

Reclaiming the feminine means honoring our bodies as sacred vessels. It means embracing the ebb and flow of our energy, emotions, and desires without judgment. It means acknowledging the pain and trauma we've experienced and holding space for healing. In this space of deep acceptance, we allow ourselves to transform, shed the layers of societal conditioning, and emerge more fully as our authentic selves.

Sacred Sexuality and the Energy Centers

There are two main energetic centers that represent sexuality: the **Sacral Chakra** and the **womb**.

The Sacral Chakra is located in the lower abdomen, just below the navel. It is associated with creativity, sexuality, emotional expression, and relationships. This chakra governs our sense of pleasure, passion, and joy, influencing how we connect with others and experience intimacy.

When balanced, the Sacral Chakra allows for healthy emotional and sexual expression, creativity, and fulfilling relationships. When blocked or out of balance, it can lead to issues like emotional instability, lack of creativity, fear of intimacy, or sexual dysfunction.

The womb is seen as a powerful, energetic, and creative center closely linked to the Sacral Chakra. Both are associated with creation—whether it's the creation of life, ideas, or personal transformation. In spiritual or energetic healing traditions, the womb can be seen as a sacred space that holds emotional and energetic imprints related to a woman's experiences, such as intimacy, creativity, and fertility.

The Journey Back to Sacred Sexuality: Three Steps

The path back to our Sacred Sexuality can be achieved through Awareness, Breath, and Self-Pleasure.

Awareness refers to the state of being conscious or mindful. It is the ability to perceive, recognize, and understand what is happening in the present moment without judgment or attachment. Bringing your awareness to your womb space and Sacral Chakra can be done with simple visualization of those spaces or by laying your hands on your body and feeling. Make a practice of bringing your awareness to your body throughout your day.

*Before beginning the following practices, creating a sacred, nurturing environment that allows you to relax and be fully present in your body is ideal. Think of these practices as sacred rituals to worship your body.

Recommendations

-Start with a relaxing bath

-Use organic oils for breast massage, like jojoba, coconut or sesame

-Light candles and/or diffuse essential oils

-Play music

Breath is a very powerful yet simple tool for reconnection.

Orb of Light Clearing Practice

- **Set Your Intention:** Begin by sitting or lying down in a comfortable, quiet space where you won't be disturbed. Close your eyes and take a few deep breaths. Set a clear intention for this practice: to love and heal yourself, to honor any feelings that arise.

- **Create Your Orb of Light:** Visualize an Orb of light in your mind's eye. This Orb can be as small as a pea or as large as a golf ball. It can be translucent or opaque, any color or shape that feels comforting and powerful to you.

- **Clear Blockages:** As the Orb moves up and down your body, visualize it absorbing or burning away any blockages, stagnant energy, or tension. Allow the Orb to dissolve any heaviness or resistance that you feel, clearing the space as it travels through you.
- **Move Through Each Chakra:** Focus your attention first on your Root Chakra, located at the base of your spine. On your next inhale, imagine the Orb of light gently rising up your spine about an inch. As you exhale, let it move down the front of your body, forming a continuous loop of energy.

- Root Chakra (base of the spine)
- Sacral Chakra (lower abdomen)
- Solar Plexus Chakra (just above the navel)
- Heart Chakra (center of your chest)
- Throat Chakra (throat area)
- Third Eye Chakra (forehead between your eyes)
- Crown Chakra (top of your head)

As you focus on each chakra, use your breath to guide the Orb through the same loop—up the spine on the inhale and down the front of the body on the exhale. Visualize the Orb clearing each chakra of stagnant energy, old emotions, or limiting beliefs.

- **Close the Practice:** Take a few final deep breaths, anchoring in the healing energy you've cultivated. When you're ready, gently open your eyes and sit in stillness, taking note of how your body feels after the practice.

Self-Pleasure

Pleasure is a potent medicine for healing. Our ability to experience pleasure is directly tied to our sense of self-worth, safety, and emotional well-being. Many women have been taught that their pleasure is secondary, or worse, that it is wrong. Reclaiming our right to experience pleasure in all its forms is essential in the journey toward living authentically.

When embraced in its fullness, pleasure creates new pathways in the brain and the body. It teaches us that we deserve to feel good, that we are worthy of receiving, and that we are not bound by the pain of the past. Self-pleasure is always available to us; we literally have access to our bodies all the time, and it is free!

Breast Massage

Breast massage is an ancient practice used to not only promote breast health but also to open the heart, awaken sexual energy, and deepen your connection with your feminine power.

Breast massage is a deeply nurturing way to honor your body and its capacity for pleasure and healing. You can connect with the energy of your heart, opening yourself to greater levels of self-love, empowerment, and authentic sexual expression.

Once you've set the space, sit or lie in a comfortable position, ensuring your body is fully supported and relaxed.

- **Begin with intention:** Place your hands over your heart and close your eyes. Take a few deep breaths and set an intention for your practice. This intention could be to open your heart, cultivate self-love, release emotional blockages, or simply experience more pleasure in your body. Breathe into this intention and feel your heart expanding with love and gratitude for yourself.

- **Warm the oil in your hands:** Take some oil into your palms and gently rub your hands together to warm the oil. Feel the warmth in your hands as a symbol of the loving, nurturing energy you are about to give yourself.

- **Start with gentle touch:** Begin by gently placing your hands over your breasts. Feel the warmth of your hands and the softness of your skin. Take a few more deep breaths, and with each inhale, imagine your breath filling your chest with love and light.

- **Circular movements:** Start massaging your breasts using gentle circular motions. Begin at the center of your chest and slowly move upward and outward, making circles around your entire breast. This direction is ideal for releasing and cleansing stuck energy.

- **Alternate directions:** After several minutes, change the direction of your circles. Start in the center of your breasts and slowly massage down and complete circles around your entire breast. This direction is ideal for energy building, love, life force, aliveness, and perkiness. *Do not massage this direction if there is anything unhealthy in your breasts.

- **Breathe and visualize:** As you massage your breasts, continue to breathe deeply. With each inhale, imagine drawing energy from the earth up into your heart. On the exhale, release any tension, stress, or emotional blockages you may be holding. You can also visualize golden light flowing through your hands and into your breasts, healing and nourishing them.

- **Connect to your body:** As you massage, focus on the sensation of your hands moving over your breasts and the energy it awakens in your heart and womb space. Imagine these spaces as a radiant, glowing center of light at the center of your chest. With each breath and each stroke, feel this light expanding, filling your chest with warmth and love.

- **Close with gratitude:** Bring your hands back to your heart once you've finished massaging. Take a few more deep breaths, feeling the energy you've cultivated through the practice. Thank your body for the pleasure and healing it provides and offer gratitude for this moment of connection with yourself.

The Seeker

I invented The Seeker, a Sacred Self-Pleasure Tool designed to support women in knowing and owning their anatomy and pleasure. I had a profound sexual experience with a partner who claimed to know my body better than me. It was both true and deeply hurtful. How could a man know my body better than me?

With a Master's Degree in Health Education, I believe I have more than average knowledge of anatomy and certainly my own body. He had triggered a spot deep inside of my vagina that activated my first-ever squirting experience. I went on a mission as a bit of a "mad scientist" to educate myself on other women's experiences, knowledge, and anatomy. What I learned was most of us have little knowledge. Why is this? Sexuality has been kept in the shadows. Most of us grew up in homes where this was not the standard dinner table conversation. Health class barely discussed pleasure or the workings of anatomy. The Seeker was born out of a *need* for women to truly explore their bodies and pleasure without the *need* for a partner.

You can combine the Orb of Light breathwork above and add your own hands, favorite sex toy, or The Seeker to amplify building pleasure and connect deeply to your body. Use your breath and the Orb as a focal point for your attention to stay present.

Reconnect to all of the parts of your body that have been in the shadows. Welcome and celebrate the connection to your body.

Surrender. Connect. Listen. Heal. Repeat as many times as you need.

With practice and intention, you can reconnect to your true, core identity, free from external influences and societal expectations, to be the most genuine and authentic version of yourself.

Integrating Sacred Sexuality into Daily Life

The practices of sacred sexuality are not limited to intimate moments or self-pleasure sessions. They can be integrated into daily life as a way of living in alignment with your authentic self. Here are some ways to bring sacred sexuality into your everyday routine:

- **Mindful Movement**
- **Sensual Living**
- **Journaling**
- **Setting Intentions**
- **Cultivating Gratitude**

By fully integrating Sacred Sexuality into your life, you create a pathway back to your authentic self. Through this reconnection to your body, emotions, and desires, you reclaim your power, heal your wounds, and live a life that is deeply aligned with who you truly are.

Sacred Sexuality is a tool for personal growth and a path back to our Divine Feminine. This is beyond the physical realm and a sacred gateway to your most authentic self, free from the constraints of societal expectations and external influences. We shift into the most powerful version of ourselves, which creates ripples in our lives, whether we are in the boardroom, the grocery store, or changing diapers!

My mission is to normalize the discussion around sexuality and women's pleasure. I believe this is a direct path to the Divine Feminine and our Authentic Selves. We are all here with a special set of gifts to share with the world, and when we are our Authentic Selves, those gifts can be shared and create the ripples that we all need to make this world the best place!

***

To contact Daphne:

www.sacredseeker.com

Louise Swartswalter

Dr. Louise Swartswalter is a speaker, transformational coach, naturopath and frequency medicine doctor, mentor and podcast host serving people around the world.

She is the creator of the **Brain Soul Success Academy and the B.R.A.I.N. System TM,** a unique multi-dimensional system that works on the mind, body, soul and energetic field all at the same time for **quicker results that stick!**

Dr. Louise Swartswalter has 30 years of experience helping people achieve optimal brain power and success in life and business. She is a *transformation* wizard blending naturopathy, NLP, Kinesiology, trauma release work and powerful energy wor*k*. She is enthusiastic about connecting; clearing blocks to success and helping others achieve their highest potential. Using a combination of tools Louise has helped people move from anxiety to calm in one session. One client told her that "one session felt like sixteen years of therapy" while another said, "she saved my life."

Her team of certified Brain Soul Success Coaches are helping people just like you worldwide transform their lives and increase their businesses. Dr. Louise has been a guest on KKOB radio and KOB-TV Good Day New Mexico and featured in Inc5000 Magazine (as a Power Partner helping other businesses) and Albuquerque Magazine top docs.

From Struggle to Triumph: The Power of the B.R.A.I.N. System™ The Brain-Soul Connection: Transforming Trauma into Triumph

By Dr. Louise Swartswalter, ND, CBS,

When we align fully with our soul's truth, our energy resonates at a higher frequency, allowing us to think clearly and make a profound impact on the world around us. One of my teachers once said, "If you're not using your gifts and letting them shine, you're dishonoring God, the divine, the universal power." This statement struck a chord deep within me, serving as a catalyst for my journey from struggle to triumph.

My journey: A Personal Testimony

I am living proof of this truth. There was a time when I battled severe allergies and three autoimmune diseases, relying on oxygen for three long years. I had panic attacks, seizures, depression, exhaustion, allergies to everything- all foods, chemicals, electricity. I had two beautiful children, and my primary goal was to be the best mother I could be. To achieve that, I needed to reclaim my health, brain power, and energy. It took me sixteen years and I had to move my family from Chicago to Taos, New Mexico to an adobe natural home to heal. I changed my diet, took my supplements, saw chiropractors, nutritionists, energy workers and I still did not feel like ME.

On my healing journey I discovered that to heal completely the physical, mental, emotional, spiritual bodies and energetic field need to be addressed "simultaneously." I was doing each piece separately and that is why it took so long to get back to ME.

Today, I know it was God's plan and I would not become the doctor, coach, speaker, and businesswoman I am today without struggle. I created The BRAIN System TM and the Brain Soul Success Academy from my path of healing my body and my life and I want to share these powerful brain hacks with you!

My first business I founded was Albuquerque National Health Center where I helped over 50,000 families in Albuquerque, NM with a variety of health issues- allergies, ADHD, auto immune imbalances, sprained ankles and more using naturopathy and biofeedback. I taught health classes and shared them on radio, TV, and local groups. I was born a teacher. I wanted to make a greater impact and teach my system, so the Brain Soul Success business I created to help entrepreneurs thrive BIG. My journey from illness to establishing multiple successful businesses fuels my passion to transform ten million brains and teach brain-soul hacks to elevate both life and business.

I believe that success in life and business for all people is achieved when you address the physical, mental, emotional, soul bodies and the energetic field simultaneously. We must clear the ancestral trauma, childhood wounds and emotions holding you back at the brain soul level and rewire your brain for success. It is the deeper inner brain soul work that reflects in the outer.

The Brain as a Master Control Tower

The brain is the master control tower of our existence. When it falters, we falter. I developed the B.R.A.I.N. System™ to address the interconnectedness of our being: Body, Release, Align, Integrate, and New Program. This system, combined with neuro biofeedback, has led to remarkable transformations for thousands of individuals and businesses.

Traditional health approaches often focus on medication, diet, and meditation, which are all crucial. However, the missing element is addressing our energy fields—releasing traumas, rewiring the brain, body, and soul. The B.R.A.I.N. System™ enables entrepreneurs to achieve greater success more rapidly by tapping into their true potential. In my thirty years of practice, I have witnessed so many beautiful, talented entrepreneurs invest so much in business courses and still not have the business or life they desire. Why? It is the inner work that reflects in the outer world. Get back to100% your soul truth and all is possible, and faster!

The Five Steps of the B.R.A.I.N. System™ B= Body, R= Release, A= Align with Spirit, I = Integrate, N= New program

1. Body: The Foundation of Health

Detox and Brain-Balancing Frequencies

Our journey begins with the body—our physical vessel. A healthy body is essential for achieving happiness, efficiency, and productivity in all aspects of life. This includes a focus on detoxification, which removes harmful substances like heavy metals and pathogens that compromise our health.

Detoxification is critical for clearing out toxins that have accumulated in our systems. From environmental pollutants to chemicals found in our everyday products, these substances can wreak havoc on our well-being. For example, research has shown that children can be born with elevated levels of toxins due to maternal exposure during pregnancy.

To support this process, we must adopt brain-boosting foods, optimize our nutrition, take essential supplements, and incorporate exercise into our daily routines. Regular sleep is non-negotiable. Without quality sleep, our brains struggle to function optimally.

Key Practices for Body Health:

- **Detoxification**: Use natural methods to cleanse the body of toxins.
- **Nutrition**: Eat a vibrant diet rich in organic fruits and vegetables and avoid processed sugars and gluten.
- **Exercise**: Engage in physical activity that suits you—yoga, tai chi, or cardiovascular workouts can all enhance brain health.
- **Sleep**: Prioritize restorative sleep to support your brain and immune system.
- **Gut Health**: Incorporate probiotics and fermented foods to nurture gut flora, which directly impacts brain function.

By adopting these practices, you set the stage for rewiring your success mechanisms.

2. Release: Letting Go of Emotional Baggage

Releasing Mental Chatter and Emotional Trauma

The next step in the B.R.A.I.N. System is to release mental and emotional traumas stored in various parts of the brain and soul. These unresolved issues can manifest as fear in the amygdala, anger in the parietal lobe, or feelings of abandonment in the cerebellum. All other emotions and the pictures of the memories get stuck in the spaces of the brain and later contribute to brain diseases such as Dementia and Parkinsons. It is the heavy metals and toxins in the physical brain coupled with childhood and ancestral trauma in the emotional brain that creates imbalances.

For instance, I once worked with a seventy-year-old woman grappling with profound grief. After losing her husband and two of her five children, we uncovered that her pain had deep roots—tracing back to her mother's death when she was just six years old. By guiding her through a process of brain-soul balancing, we were able to release this long-held grief, allowing her to live fully again.

Healing transcends mere forgiveness; it requires acceptance of past experiences. Your parents did the best they could with the tools they had at their disposal. This understanding can bring immense relief and set the stage for true healing.

3. Align: Connecting with Higher Frequencies

Align Spiritually to Attract Success and Prosperity

The alignment phase involves soul clearing and rebooting your energy field with the new program that reflects your aspirations—be it improved health, deeper relationships, or greater success.

Here is one my favorite meditations to help you align with spirit:

1. Ground – Imagine sending roots out from the bottom of your feet, going deep down to the center of force Earth. Imagine wrapping your roots around elements of gold, rubies, or diamonds.
2. Align – Imagine the power and force of Earth's energy coming into your body and align your heart to that force. Breathe in and out.

3. Go to theta – Imagine a golden laser beam of light coming down into you from above and going through you down below you into the Earth. Travel on this bolt of light outer regions of galaxies and beyond. Pass the stars until you are in black void of space and into white luminescence of source. This is the place of creation of all that you desire.

4. Command – I do not know how ______________________________. I only know that I do now, and I am fulfilled. (Make statements in now.)

5. Expand - Apply simple and powerful techniques – Expand the vision that serves better than the original idea.

6. Receive with Gratitude – Move consciousness back down the golden beam of light into your physical body and imagine the particles of consciousness of your manifestation floating down from Source Energy into the cells of your body and your DNA itself. Imagine unwinding, unwinding the old limiting ideas and rewinding a new holographic image of this life that is your new life. Feel it, accept it, and give thanks. Thank you. It is done. So be it! Take a deep breath and send your energy down into the Earth to firmly establish your ground of being.

Start with, I do not know how ____________________. I only know it is so now, and I am fulfilled.

Theta Meditation:

https://drive.google.com/file/d/18qhMZni9EG9UbTR8mo4Y3iyEtITH-gpj/view?usp=sharing

4. Integrate: Unifying Mind and Spirit

Integrate Your Soul's New Frequencies with Your True Purpose

The "I" in the B.R.A.I.N. System focuses on integrating your soul's new brain frequencies. This vital step involves transforming old ancestral patterns and connecting with past ancestors. By releasing these outdated programs, you create a harmonious life that aligns with your true purpose.

Connecting with your ancestral lineage can provide insights into patterns that may be affecting your current life. By understanding and integrating these lessons, you can forge a path toward a more fulfilling existence.

5. New Program: Installing Positive Patterns

The last step in the B.R.A.I.N. System is about creating a new program for health and vitality. This phase empowers you to install positive, life-affirming patterns through energy work and meditation.

Utilizing these practices, you can overcome old habits and create a vibrant, empowered version of yourself. The new program includes the success codes that change all four lobes of the brain by addressing the brain rings- think quantum physics and energy combined. The old patterns are transmuted and allow your gift to shine. The codes clear seven generations back and seven forward. Yes, my own kids who were teenagers at the time I learned the codes shifted through the work I did on myself. I remember coming home from that weekend class and thinking what happened while I was gone? Both my kids were different.

The Importance of Addressing Trauma

Trauma can profoundly affect our well-being, even influencing aspects like fertility. Stress and trauma create energetic blockages that can hinder our ability to conceive or maintain a healthy state.

For example, I worked with a client who experienced a miscarriage. After addressing the unresolved emotions linked to that loss, she became pregnant again, free from the weight of past grief. This is why it is crucial to clear these energies as soon as possible, allowing for healing and progress.

Stories to share.

We learn through other people's stories. By learning the B.R.A.I.N. System, countless individuals have experienced profound transformations. Here is the story of an event a client shared.

In the heart of the serene retreat center, the air hummed with the energy of shared experiences and collective healing. This was no ordinary gathering; it was a sanctuary where souls converged, each carrying their own burdens yet ready to shed them. Dr. Louise stood at the forefront, guiding her group through a journey of discovery and empowerment.

Lana stepped forward, her energy vibrant. "I have released thirty-four pounds without dieting! Can you believe it?" The room erupted in supportive cheers. "But it is more than just the weight. I have transformed my grief into empowerment. The practice partners I have worked with have been incredible. I feel lighter in my body and spirit. The stress is melting away and I got my courage back and started sailing." As she spoke, her smile radiated confidence, a beacon of hope for those still navigating their own struggles.

Lezli, a remarkable testament to resilience, followed Lana. "My journey began with a traumatic brain injury," she began, her tone earnest. "But Dr. Louise did not just treat my symptoms; she guided me to understand the root cause—a brain lesion from a past event. Now, I am free from vertigo and anxiety. I have even started a new career!" Her eyes sparkled with renewed purpose. "The support from this mastermind group has been invaluable. I have learned to enrich my family relationships and rebuild my life. It is a miracle."

As Lezli spoke, Dr. Mary nodded, adding her own experience to the tapestry. "I had been struggling with Epstein Barr, missing work for months. But the techniques I learned here changed everything. I have embraced love and released the emotional guard I built over the years. My business has flourished alongside my health, and I feel lighter, more alive than ever."

Dr. Pat, a medical physician, chimed in, sharing her own transformation. "Dr. Louise's approach is unlike anything I have encountered. She's taught me to clear negativity from my energetic field, and now, I respond to life with positivity and care. I feel at peace, and my self-worth has soared."

Bonnie's story flowed next, revealing the depth of her journey. "After 30 years in ministry, I finally retired to pursue my passion for healing retreats and energy work. In just four months, I have gained eight new clients and facilitated a healing weekend that had eluded me for years." Her eyes shone with purpose, igniting inspiration in everyone around her.

Laurene concluded the sharing, her voice filled with newfound conviction. "I had been battling hormonal imbalances and anxiety for years, visiting countless doctors without answers. This group has taught me to trust my intuition and clear energies that do not belong to me. I am not just healing myself; I am able to help others."

As each story unfolded, the collective energy in the room surged, weaving together threads of struggle, triumph, and transformation. Dr. Louise observed with a heart full of joy. This was what she had envisioned—a tapestry of healing where everyone's journey contributed to the greater whole.

"Together, you are a force of nature," she said, her voice resonating with warmth. "Each of you has faced challenges, and each of you has emerged stronger, more empowered. This is just the beginning of your journey. Keep sharing, keep healing, and keep shining."

With that, the group erupted in applause, a chorus of celebration for the transformations they had witnessed in one another. The energy shifted, blossoming into a profound sense of community, trust, and hope. They had come seeking answers, and what they found was so much more: a family of souls committed to growth and healing.

As the session ended, Lana, Lezli, Dr. Mary, Dr. Pat, Bonnie, and Laurene left the room, not just as individuals but as a united force, ready to take on the world with newfound confidence and strength.

Final Thoughts

I went from a frail eighty-nine pounds, reliant on an oxygen tank, to a thriving entrepreneur earning millions. The B.R.A.I.N. System TM played an integral role in this transformation, and I am excited to share these tools with you.

If I can do it, so can you.

- **B = Body**: Focus on detoxification and nutrition.
- **R = Release**: Let go of mental and emotional baggage.
- **A = Align**: Connect spiritually to raise your frequency.
- **I = Integrate**: Harmonize your mind with your soul's purpose.

- **N = New Program**: Create a vibrant program of health and vitality.

The B.R.A.I.N. System TM is not just a method; it is a transformative journey. By addressing the complete system simultaneously, you will gain the tools to achieve success in health, life, and business.

Let this be your moment of transformation. The power lies within you.

Our yearlong Mastermind and our Brain Soul Success Academy is the most comprehensive transformational program for entrepreneurs and business owners. Our clients achieve miracles -make more money, author books. get more clients, get super healthy, gain confidence, release addictions and more.

Learning Brain Soul hacks allows our clients to " Take Back their Power." Our events, masterclasses and podcast, The Brain Soul Success Show empower individuals to act and finally allow their gifts to shine!

***

To contact Louise:

I invite you to delve deeper into the B.R.A.I.N. System. Visit my website, www.louiseswartswalter.com
and www.brainsoulsuccess.com

Together, we can determine your best next steps toward achieving your goals.

Our Free Brain Soul Assessment is an opportunity to meet with a Success Coach and discover your biggest brain block to your success. https://louiseswartswalter.com/brain-soul-assessment/

Get our five-minute brain hack and begin your journey today.

Mind Gems: https://louiseswartswalter.com/mindgemsgift/

Listen the Brain Soul Success Show podcast:
https://podcasts.apple.com/us/podcast/brain-soul-success-show/id1538654652

Find us on social media:

Facebook: https://www.facebook.com/louise.swartswalter

Instagram https://www.instagram.com/drlouiseswartswalter/

YouTube https://www.youtube.com/user/abqnaturalhealth

Linked In https://www.linkedin.com/in/louise-swartswalter-330174a/

Michal Ofer

Michal Ofer is a highly sought-after nutrition and lifestyle consultant, specializing in a functional medicine approach that prioritizes healing through nutrition and optimizing overall well-being. Her philosophy is rooted in a "nutrition-first" and "protein-centric" model, recognizing that real, whole foods, especially high-quality protein, are the foundation of sustainable health, energy, and vitality.

Michal designs tailored, practical nutrition plans that not only meet your unique health goals but also focus on nutrient density and the critical role of protein in supporting metabolic function, muscle maintenance, hormone balance, and immune health. Her expertise lies in identifying and addressing the barriers and roadblocks that hinder clients from achieving peak health potential, offering strategic and individualized solutions for overcoming these challenges.

With a degree in Life Sciences and certification as a Master Life Coach, Michal brings a comprehensive and compassionate approach to her work. She has received extensive training and accreditation from multiple respected nutrition institutions and is dedicated to ongoing education by attending, presenting, and participating in conferences, workshops, and seminars worldwide.

Michal regularly publishes content on multiple platforms, sharing her expertise in personalized nutrition strategies, functional wellness, and protein-centric meal plans. She is also actively involved in private and corporate recipe development, helping individuals and businesses embrace a whole-foods approach that nourishes the body on a cellular level and promotes long-term well-being.

Protein - Your Key To Living Long & Well"

By Michal Ofer

In today's world, health has become more complex than ever before. We are constantly bombarded with information on what to eat, how to exercise, and which supplements to take. Yet, with all this noise, people are still struggling to feel their best, and many are further from optimal health than they've ever been. The key, as I've learned through decades of research, coaching, and personal experience, lies in one of the most fundamental building blocks of life: protein.

Protein is not just a macronutrient—it's the foundation of human health. It influences everything from muscle growth and fat loss to brain function, energy levels, and even longevity. Yet, many people don't fully understand the critical role it plays in shaping their well-being.

This isn't just about eating more protein; it's about eating the right proteins in the right amounts at the right times. Throughout my career, I've worked with thousands of individuals to fine-tune their diets, helping them thrive by aligning their food choices with their bodies' natural needs. From athletes to professionals to busy parents, I've seen the profound changes that occur when protein intake is optimized—greater energy, leaner bodies, sharper minds, and a renewed sense of vitality.

Protein is your secret weapon whether you're looking to lose weight, build muscle, enhance your cognitive function, or simply live a longer, healthier life.

This isn't a one-size-fits-all approach. As you'll see, the path to optimal health is deeply personal, and I'll guide you in customizing your protein intake to suit your individual goals and needs. My mission is simple: to empower you with the knowledge and tools to take control of your health, starting with one of our most powerful levers—protein.

The Essential Role of Protein in Human Physiology

In the world of nutrition, protein often takes a back seat to other macronutrients, misunderstood or overshadowed by trendy diet advice and conflicting views on fat and carbohydrates. But at its core, protein is arguably the most vital macronutrient for sustaining life, growth, and health. Every cell in your body relies on protein to function, repair, and thrive. It's not just a building block for muscles—it's the foundation of your body's physiological processes, from hormone production to immune defense.

What is Protein?

Protein is made up of long chains of amino acids, often referred to as the "building blocks of life." These amino acids perform countless essential functions in the body, from constructing tissues to synthesizing enzymes and hormones. Nine of the 20 amino acids are classified as *essential*, meaning the body cannot produce them and must be obtained through diet. These essential amino acids play critical roles in processes like muscle repair, brain function, and metabolic regulation.

The body continuously breaks down and rebuilds proteins, especially in muscle, skin, and organs. We need a regular supply of dietary protein to keep these processes running smoothly. Without adequate intake, the body starts to break down its own muscle tissue to meet its protein needs, leading to muscle wasting, impaired immune function, and poor overall health.

Protein's Core Functions in the Body

Building and Repairing Tissues

One of protein's most well-known functions is its role in building and repairing tissues. Whether you're recovering from an injury, working out to build muscle, or simply going about your daily life, your body constantly requires protein to repair and regenerate damaged cells. Every organ, from your skin to your heart, relies on protein to maintain its structure and function. Muscle repair and growth, in particular, depend heavily on adequate protein intake, making it a key focus for anyone looking to improve their strength, endurance, or physical performance.

Supporting Immune Function

Proteins are also essential for immune function. Antibodies, which protect the body from harmful invaders like viruses and bacteria, are made up of proteins. A protein deficiency can impair the immune system, making it harder for the body to fight off infections and recover from illness. Protein should be a cornerstone of your nutrition plan if your goal is to build resilience and reduce your risk of illness.

Enzyme Production and Metabolic Regulation

Enzymes, which are responsible for carrying out the chemical reactions that sustain life, are proteins. These enzymes help break down food, produce energy, and synthesize the molecules your body needs to function. Enzyme production can become compromised without sufficient protein, leading to metabolic dysfunctions. Protein also regulates hormones like insulin and growth hormone, which are critical for energy metabolism, cell growth, and recovery.

Transporting Nutrients and Oxygen

Hemoglobin, the protein responsible for transporting oxygen in the blood, is another example of how deeply protein is woven into your body's essential processes. Proteins also act as carriers for important vitamins and minerals, helping to shuttle these nutrients where they are needed most. For example, transferrin, a transport protein, binds to iron and ensures its delivery to your cells for use in energy production and immune function.

Maintaining Fluid and pH Balance

Proteins help regulate the balance of fluids in your body by maintaining the proper distribution of water between tissues and blood vessels. They also play a key role in maintaining acid-base balance, which is crucial for normal cellular function. A diet deficient in protein can lead to issues with fluid retention, swelling, and disruptions in pH levels, making it harder for your body to function optimally.

Why Protein Should Be the Foundation of Your Nutrition Plan

With so many essential functions, it's clear that protein is not simply another macronutrient—it's a critical nutrient for survival and optimal health. Unfortunately, many modern diets fall short of providing adequate protein, focusing instead on cutting calories, fats, or carbs without considering the consequences of protein deficiency. Prioritizing protein should be at the heart of any nutrition strategy.

The Foundation of Every Cell

Every cell, tissue, and organ in your body relies on protein for its structure and function. It's not just your muscles that need protein—your enzymes, hormones, and immune system are all dependent on a steady supply of high-quality amino acids.

When you don't get enough protein, your body lacks the raw materials needed for cellular repair, immune defense, and metabolic processes. Over time, this can lead to fatigue, weight gain, muscle loss, poor recovery, and an increased risk of chronic diseases. Simply put, without enough protein, your body can't thrive.

Supports Lean Muscle Mass & Fat Loss

Protein is essential for building and preserving lean muscle mass, especially as you age.

One of the most misunderstood aspects of protein is its role in fat loss. Contrary to popular belief, losing weight isn't just about cutting calories—it's about maintaining muscle mass and metabolic health. Protein is your best ally because of its role in:

Muscle Preservation: When you lose weight, you risk losing muscle along with fat, especially if you're on a low-protein diet. Losing muscle slows down your metabolism, making it harder to keep the weight off. Adequate protein intake helps preserve lean muscle, keeping your metabolism higher even as you shed fat.

Thermic Effect of Food (TEF): Protein has a high thermic effect, requiring more energy to digest than fats and carbohydrates. In other words, you burn more calories simply by eating more protein. This makes it a metabolic advantage in weight loss.

Appetite Regulation: Protein is the most satiating macronutrient. It signals fullness and reduces cravings, helping you naturally control your calorie intake without feeling deprived.

By prioritizing protein, you're fueling fat loss and setting your body up for long-term success by preserving muscle and maintaining metabolic health.

Supports Tissue Repair and Immune Function

Whether you're recovering from an intense workout, surgery, or illness, protein is the crucial nutrient your body relies on to repair tissues and recover quickly. Athletes, active individuals, and anyone recovering from trauma or surgery will benefit from increasing their protein intake to accelerate healing and reduce inflammation.

Protein also provides the amino acids necessary for immune function. Amino acids, especially those found in high-quality animal proteins, are vital for the synthesis of enzymes, hormones, and antibodies that protect the body from infection and inflammation. Amino acids such as glutamine play a crucial role in gut health, which is integral to controlling inflammation and immune regulation. By supporting tissue repair and immune function, protein can prevent chronic inflammation, which is a key driver of many diseases, including heart disease and cancer.

Promotes Cardiovascular Health

Contrary to outdated beliefs, higher-protein diets can promote cardiovascular health. Protein helps maintain healthy blood pressure, supports arterial function, and regulates lipid metabolism. Optimizing protein intake can help manage blood pressure, cholesterol, and triglyceride levels by promoting healthier body composition and reducing inflammation.

Anti-Inflammatory Benefits

Many chronic diseases, including autoimmune conditions, arthritis, and even cancer, are driven by chronic inflammation. Protein, especially from high-quality sources, helps rebuild tissues while controlling inflammation through the balance of essential amino acids and fats.

Hormone Regulation

Proteins are the precursors to many hormones that regulate vital processes, including insulin, thyroid, and growth hormones. Adequate protein intake helps restore hormonal balance, improve energy levels, and support metabolic health. Hormonal imbalances can lead to weight gain, mood disorders, fatigue, and various metabolic problems.

Cognitive Function and Mental Health

Your brain relies on protein to produce neurotransmitters like serotonin, dopamine, and acetylcholine, which are vital for mood regulation, focus, memory, and overall cognitive function. Optimizing protein intake can help improve symptoms of depression, anxiety, and cognitive decline by ensuring your brain has the raw materials it needs for optimal neurotransmitter production and brain function.

Protein also supports brain health by stabilizing blood sugar levels and preventing energy crashes that can lead to brain fog and poor mental clarity.

Bone Health

Protein works alongside calcium and vitamin D to maintain bone density and strength. Contrary to the myth that high-protein diets are bad for bones, research shows that protein supports bone mineralization and reduces the risk of fractures, especially in older adults.

Enhances Metabolic Health and Insulin Sensitivity

Adequate protein intake improves metabolic health by promoting insulin sensitivity and blood sugar regulation. For individuals struggling with insulin resistance or type 2 diabetes, a diet rich in high-quality protein can help restore balance, prevent blood sugar spikes, and reduce the risk of metabolic syndrome.

Supports Longevity

While many think of protein as something needed only by athletes or bodybuilders, it's equally essential for anyone who wants to age gracefully and remain active into their later years. Studies show that individuals who maintain higher levels of muscle mass and strength throughout life tend to live longer and have a better quality of life. Protein supports the maintenance of lean tissue, brain health, and immune function, all contributing to longevity. Prioritizing protein is one of the most effective ways to age gracefully, prevent chronic diseases, and maintain vitality into your later years.

How Much Protein Do You Actually Need?

Despite its importance, most people under-consume protein, especially as they age. Traditional dietary guidelines often underestimate protein requirements, leading many to fall short. To truly optimize health, it's critical to understand that **more protein is often better.**

The minimum recommended dietary allowance (RDA) for protein—0.8 grams per kilogram of body weight (0.36 grams per pound)—is designed to prevent deficiency, not to promote optimal health. For most individuals, especially those looking to lose fat, gain muscle, or age well, a more effective target is between **1.6 and 2.2 grams of protein per kilogram of body weight (0.8 to 1.0 grams per pound).**

This means that if you weigh 70 kg (about 154 pounds), you should aim for at least 112 to 154 grams of protein per day. This higher protein intake ensures you're getting enough to maintain muscle, support your immune system, and optimize metabolic health.

Quality Matters

Not all proteins are created equal. The quality of your protein—measured by its amino acid profile and bioavailability—matters just as much as the quantity. Animal-based proteins, such as meat, fish, eggs, and dairy, contain all nine essential amino acids in the correct ratios, making them the most complete and bioavailable sources.

However, while valuable, plant-based proteins are often incomplete and less bioavailable. If you follow a plant-based diet, combining different protein sources (like beans, grains, and seeds) to ensure you're getting all essential amino acids is essential. Supplementing with a high-quality protein powder may also be necessary to meet your protein needs.

Timing and Distribution of Protein

Equally important is how much protein you consume, when, and how you consume it. Studies suggest that spreading protein intake evenly across meals is more effective for muscle protein synthesis than consuming a large portion at once. Aim to include at least 30 grams or more of protein at each meal to maximize muscle repair, recovery, and growth. This is particularly important at your first and last meals of the day.

The Power of Personalization

One of the most exciting developments in nutrition science is the realization that protein needs are highly individual. Factors like age, gender, activity level, and health goals all influence how much protein you need to thrive. For example:

Athletes and active individuals require more protein to support muscle repair and recovery.

Older adults benefit from increased protein to combat muscle loss and maintain strength.

Those looking to lose fat can use a high-protein diet to preserve muscle and promote fat loss.

Protein is the cornerstone of a healthy, strong body, but how much you need is unique to you. Factors such as your age, activity level, body composition, and health goals all play a role in determining your ideal protein intake. A sedentary person with minimal muscle mass will need a different protein intake than an athlete focused on building muscle or an individual trying to lose weight while preserving lean tissue. While protein is the foundation, many other factors must be considered to optimize body composition, heal inflammation, reverse chronic conditions, and prevent future health issues.

To personalize your protein intake:

Assess Your Current Body Composition: Understanding your lean body mass versus fat mass is crucial. Those with more muscle require more protein for maintenance and growth, while individuals with higher body fat may benefit from increasing protein to support fat loss without losing muscle.

Factor in Activity Level: Your daily activity level greatly influences protein requirements. More active individuals—especially those engaging in strength training, endurance exercise, or high-intensity workouts—need higher protein to repair and rebuild muscle tissue. Athletes may benefit from consuming 2.0–2.5 grams of protein per kilogram of body weight, while less active individuals can aim for 1.6–2.0 grams.

Adjust for Age: As we age, we become more prone to muscle loss (sarcopenia). Increasing protein intake can help counteract this, promoting muscle retention and reducing the risk of frailty. Older adults should aim for higher protein per meal, ensuring each one contains **at least** 30–40 grams to stimulate muscle protein synthesis effectively.

Consider Metabolic Health: If you're managing insulin resistance, type 2 diabetes, or other metabolic conditions, protein can play a key role in regulating blood sugar and supporting healthy weight management. Prioritize lean, high-quality protein sources and distribute them evenly throughout the day to help stabilize blood sugar and prevent energy crashes.

By tailoring your protein intake to your unique needs, you can unlock greater levels of health, performance, and longevity. However, your journey to optimal health is unique; your diet should reflect that. Here's how to bring it all together:

Start with Protein: Determine your ideal protein intake based on your body composition, activity level, and health goals. Ensure you're getting high-quality protein at every meal.

Tailor Your Carb and Fat Intake: Adjust your intake of healthy fats and nutrient-dense carbohydrates (from real food sources like vegetables and fruits) based on your energy needs, metabolism, and fat loss or muscle gain goals.

Embrace Whole Foods: Focus on nutrient-dense, whole foods that promote healing and reduce inflammation. This includes the best quality meats, fish, vegetables, and healthy, naturally occurring fats like animal fats, olive oil, and avocado oil.

Listen to Your Body: Personalization is a dynamic process. As you make changes to your diet, pay attention to how your body responds. Track how you feel, your energy levels, digestion, and any signs of inflammation. Adjust your protein intake, food choices, and meal timing based on your evolving needs.

Monitor Your Progress: Regularly assess your body composition, health markers, and overall well-being. Whether you're using body fat measurements, blood tests, or simply tracking how you look, feel, and perform, keeping tabs on your progress will help you fine-tune your approach.

Unlocking Your Health Potential

Protein is so much more than a nutrient—it's the foundation of your health, the key to longevity, and a powerful agent for healing and preventing disease. Protein is the key to everything—from achieving your ideal body composition to living disease-free to aging with vitality. By optimizing your protein intake and personalizing it to fit your body and lifestyle, you unlock the full potential of your health. Armed with this knowledge, you have the power to take control of your health and build the blueprint for a life where you can thrive, age gracefully, and protect yourself from the chronic conditions that plague so many.

As you move forward, I encourage you to make protein the priority in your nutrition plan, regardless of where you are on your health journey. This isn't simply about hitting a protein target—it's about living with intention, nourishing your body deeply, and stepping into the healthiest, strongest version of yourself. Let protein guide you as you continue to unlock more significant levels of vitality, longevity, and resilience, one meal at a time.

***

Michal can be reached at:

http://michalofer.com

Email: info@michalofer.com

Facebook: http://facebook.com/MichalOfer.LifestyleWellness

Instagram: @ofermichal

X: @MichalOfer

LinkedIn: Michal Ofer

Helen Eimers

Helen is an experienced online coach and entrepreneur who has empowered hundreds of women to boost their energy, influence, and income. With nearly a decade in the coaching industry, her heartfelt support and honest guidance help midlife entrepreneurs build the businesses of their dreams.

Before launching Amplify Academy, Helen had a 16-year nursing career, excelling in case management and program development for a multimillion-dollar woman-owned company. Her transition into entrepreneurship not only replaced her nursing income but also set the stage for her thriving coaching business.

As a nationally recognized speaker, Helen is known for her captivating presence and passion for her mission. Her diverse skill set, which includes her training as a Registered Nurse, hypnotherapist, yoga instructor, and healer, allows her to provide a nurturing and empowering space for her clients to thrive.

Helen lives in rural South Dakota with her husband and three children, enjoying the strong community ties that surround her. Summers are spent along the Missouri River in Chamberlain, where she blends her love of nature with teaching yoga and paddleboard yoga, creating a unique and adventurous experience for her students.

You are the gift

By Helen Eimers

During a hypnotherapy session, I encountered my mother as a four-year-old. I envisioned and felt myself nestled into her lap, my head resting on her chest. Her warm, soft body and arms wrapped around me. I was feeling safe, warm, and surrounded by love.

My mom had something for me. A gift. But at first there was nothing. I tried harder to connect and longed to see what she had to share, but then I started to doubt there was anything there.

Then it came.

Slowly, she pulled out a mirror and held it in front of my face. I began to shake with sobs as I realized what she was showing me. Her message. No words were necessary.

Her gift was me.

This was a profound realization.

To experience my mother in this way was the ultimate gift. I was just four when my mother, Darlene, died in a tragic car accident. Her sudden absence left a gaping hole in my life.

That tragic loss has become an incredible opportunity for healing.

I long for her to be here, but I know now that she still is.

This gift, her gifts, still present themselves in my life every day. She is still teaching, showing, and guiding me.

When you finish reading this chapter, I want you to feel some of the relief, joy, peace and hope I felt that day in my hypnotherapy session. I want you to discover the freedom of the truth that is waiting to be revealed.

My whole life I searched for another answer - something bigger than me, something outside of me, more elaborate or profound. Had I received this message any earlier in my life, I would have thought it was too simple.

But, in the depths of a hypnotherapy session, my mom shared this message with me: 'You are the gift.' It was as if that moment and that message had been planned long before she left this earth.

She didn't have to say it. She simply showed me and I knew.

I arrived at this place of peace, joy, deep love, and gratitude after ten years of mindfulness and intentional work. Every part of who I am and my perfectly imperfect story prepared me to be able to receive that gift.

My journey to self-discovery and awareness was guided by those I love. In their own ways, they each helped open my eyes to the over-stimulated, stressed, angry, burnt out life I was living.

Helping and saving was instilled in my heart at a young age. My dad modeled a spirit of giving, pride, and passion with his too-numerous-to-count volunteer hours.

These deeply rooted values guided me towards a career in nursing. I spent 15 years supporting patients from their first breath to their last and everywhere in between.

It is my passion and purpose to help others.

I poured myself into work of all kinds. From the time I was 11, I don't recall a time when I didn't have at least two jobs. I was always working, giving, staying late and volunteering. I was eager to learn and take on everything, going in early and picking up extra shifts to prove it.

After four years of learning, growing, and advancing as a nurse, I found myself drifting further from the woman I longed to be. My emotions reared up each and every day. The inability to control them and 'figure it out' was exhausting.

I found myself screaming at my kids to be happy, longing for the hour they would go to sleep so I could relax. Showing up to work, I felt resentful and frustrated, certain I was the only one who cared. I spent my time immersed in the gossip of my coworkers to validate myself and build my ego.

On the weekends, when I wasn't working, I would buffer with alcohol to let loose. After too much, I would feel extreme guilt and shame. I was on a repeat reel, telling myself never again, yet finding myself in the same spot the following week.

I took pride in my marriage and told everyone it was perfect because we never fought. The truth was, I couldn't handle an adult conversation with my husband without my emotions feeling too out of control and losing my shit – so I avoided the conversations altogether.

Behind the giving, helping, passionate nurse, mother, wife, daughter, friend, and coworker,

I slowly started to realize the pain, hurt, anger, guilt, shame, and pure exhaustion behind the beautiful picture I painted for myself and others.

The work of hiding from myself was exhausting. I desperately tried to fill the cracks in my life with overworking, over-consuming, distractions, and forced happiness. Eventually, the cracks started to open wider, shifting to deep, dark crevices.

I was angry, bitter, judgmental, jaded and spiteful.

For years, I couldn't see it happening. I couldn't see myself sliding further and further into avoidance, burnout, and evasion of my feelings.

I told myself I was fine. I focused on the reality of happiness. I only allowed positive emotions into my life, my heart and my relationships. I battled negative emotions fiercely. But they didn't go away. These emotions burrowed even deeper into the cracks that were opening up. Negative emotions were bad, not something I wanted in my life. There was one path to life and that was happiness.

Yet, in my persistent pursuit of fierce happiness, my husband asked me a shocking question.

"When will you ever be happy?"

"I am happy!" I screamed in response… but my entire physical body screamed otherwise. He could see that, deep down, there was fear. He could see the ways I avoided any negative emotion, which actually made me experience more of it on the inside - bottling it up and carrying it all on my own. I thought I was protecting myself and everyone else from the pain of it. The narrow path of manufactured happiness I was forcing myself down created suffocation.

I was fine. I was successful. I had the house, the kids, the job, the friends, the social life. I was so passionate. I was helping so many people and doing the right thing – exactly what I was supposed to do.

The reality was, I was burning myself out at work to avoid looking inward. I was avoiding the hard conversations because I didn't want to feel the pain. I was the hype cheerleader in every situation, dodging negative emotions within myself and others.

What I had yet to learn was that the emotions we refuse to feel never go away. They fester, growing deeper and darker until the moment when the cracks open wide, and the ground loses all stability.

The spiraling was happening so fast within me, I couldn't see what was going on. It was like trying to catch a glimpse of an animal through the side window while driving 80 miles per hour. I just kept driving.

Truly, I was living a blessed and fruitful life. My life was full of abundance and joy. While I was grateful, there was a deeper level of gratitude and love all around me, and I longed to feel it.

I vividly recall the day my husband returned home from a conference with a personal development book. He excitedly told me about the speaker and purchased a book thinking I might like to read it. You can imagine my excitement around this 'gift' when my ego was the star of the show. I didn't need 'help.' Everything was fine.

But it wasn't.

It took time, but I slowly started to read the book. My heart and mind started to open up in new and exciting ways as I took in the concepts. I began to change little parts of my days instead of trying to change my whole life all at once. Unlike the frustration, overwhelm, guilt, and shame I experienced in the past, this felt manageable. It felt doable. And that alone felt really, really good.

Mindfulness entered my perspective. Instead of rushing through life, trying to do more and be more, I became aware. I noticed the thoughts I was thinking, the words I was using and realized the stories I had created.

So many untrue stories were deeply ingrained into who I was, how I showed up and the ways I lived my life. I had created and believed them as a form of protection.

I am not a morning person.

Everyone should be happy all the time.

Busy is a status symbol.

I have to prove myself.

I have to save others.

No one can do it as well as I can.

I kept reading and learning. Soon, I became obsessed with the reality of who I was at the core. I began a journey to discover and love myself.

With each awareness of the unhealthy habits, I had fallen into and the thoughts that guided those actions, there was an emotional connection. I felt hurt and pain, but the guilt, shame, and anger towards myself continued to soften.

Each day, I became more keenly aware that making changes from a place of hate, anger, guilt, shame, and fear created incredible resistance. It kept me from the future I longed for. It made new habits difficult, if not impossible, to adopt.

When I started to take action towards my future self with love, compassion, kindness, and encouragement, the work felt lighter.

I felt myself shift from surviving to thriving in my work - taking on more than I ever had in the past but feeling a lightness and love around it. I showed up with more love and kindness towards myself and that permeated into every person I came into contact with.

It was a genuineness and authenticity that I had never experienced. It felt like my True Self.

I started going to therapy when I was in my 30s, after my grandfather passed away. All the emotions surrounding that situation felt too heavy to bear. Why couldn't I handle this? I was a strong woman. I was accomplished. I had never needed therapy before.

I will never forget two questions my therapist asked me.

"Are you taking any drugs?"

"Have you ever had therapy since your mother passed away?"

The first question stemmed from the incredibly superhuman way I was only sleeping four hours a night and functioning from the outside as a successful professional nurse, entrepreneur, mother, wife and fitness enthusiast. I worked and buffered and drove myself into complete exhaustion to avoid my emotions.

The second question came straight from her heart, imagining the hurt and pain after such a tragic loss at such a fragile age.

My answer to both was no.

She shed light on my thoughts. She sat quietly as I processed. She didn't judge me when I told her I hated the way she stayed silent as the words and tears bubbled out of me. Unfazed, she held space for me to feel all of it.

There was so much pain, hate, hurt, fear, and anger that flowed out. It felt awful.

But afterward, I felt a lightness.

And most importantly, I felt.

I had never fully allowed myself – or those around me – to feel negative emotions.

My whole life, the most heartfelt people had been trying to save me from my pain, so I did that too. As humans, it is our innate nature to protect ourselves and others from pain. We are fierce in our efforts.

This saving mindset was ingrained deep within me and led me to my career in nursing where I loved caring for, comforting, and holding space for patients and families. When I was doing this for others, my own fears melted away.

Allowing myself to feel and process through emotions was new for me. Instead of trying to dodge my fear, hurt, anger, jealousy, guilt, shame, and loneliness, I took time to feel them.

I started to realize there was nothing wrong with me. I was not broken.

I was human.

I was worthy. I was a gift.

This realization was an incredible shift in who I was at my core.

I started to show up for myself and others as someone who encouraged instead of judged.

I shifted my energy from saving to supporting, releasing all the pressure and control I had tried so hard to micromanage.

Everything felt lighter, more free, more peaceful.

I opened my heart to forgive myself and others. No longer holding onto the anger, hate, the 'karma will get you' attitude and self-loathing.

I connected with old friends and said, 'I'm sorry.'

I became mindful of the thoughts and words that rolled through my mind and out of my mouth.

I sought out professionals for support.

The lies I created, believed, and lived for most of my life started to shift. I showed up with the energy that I truly was worthy and capable of my reality.

I was no longer a victim of my circumstances.

The belief that 'I am not a morning person' created hours of snoozing, a bitter morning atmosphere and being absent as a mother at this time of day.

The belief that 'I am the only one that can do this properly' led me to never saying no or allowing others to help. I did things myself from a spirit of anger and spite.

The work I have done for 10 years, and continue to do daily, includes practicing awareness, gratitude and intentional thoughts.

For most of my life, I was laser focused on what was going wrong, what was lacking, what I could create a commiserating conversation around. The juicier the better.

Once I started to practice gratitude daily, my eyes opened to the beautiful blessings all around me. I began to notice abundance, peace, and opportunities. It was a daily conversation of prayer.

Each day, I consume positivity and learning. I read personal development books – everything from self-worth to creating a millionaire mindset – along with online courses, training, webinars, and programs.

Investing in myself with a supportive and encouraging coach was the catalyst for shifting my business from a hobby to an incredibly successful dream job.

My past self-defined success as a status symbol, climbing the corporate ladder, being the most seen, heard, important person in the room. Being busy and a step above everyone.

Today, I have a pretty unique definition of success.

Success is putting one foot in front of the other. Getting back up when you fall down. Facing your deepest fears and most terrifying emotions. It's saying, 'I'm sorry' and 'thank you.' It is sitting quietly and listening without the intent to respond when someone shares hard things. It's when you are able to own your wrongs. The ultimate definition of success is when you can look directly in the mirror, see your reflection and fiercely, honestly, with tears in your eyes and a vibration in your heart say, "I love you."

This shift in my perception of success has come from introspective work like journaling, meditation, visualization, and hypnotherapy.

When you infuse this work into your life, anything is possible because you have chosen to make it possible.

I love to teach the strategy side, helping women create an action plan and get big, bold results. However, without the thoughts and emotions that support the work and the belief that you can make it happen, there will be resistance.

This resistance is ultimately a form of protection from negative emotion. The most powerful thing I do for myself, and my clients, is facilitate awareness, love, and acknowledgement of these emotions, followed by a conscious heart choice forward.

And because these choices are available and waiting for all of us, I am fierce in the way I support and encourage others toward this beautiful reality of success in their lives.

For the past ten years, I have shown up every day for myself and others with joy, positivity, gratitude, humbleness, and encouragement.

At first, it will feel like more work and commitment to take time to dive inward. And it is; learning new things, challenging yourself each day, being consistent, making a choice to not watch another episode of your latest Netflix binge is hard.

But.

The cycle of survival is far more exhausting than stepping into the fear of doing new and hard things or growing or evolving.

My whole being comes alive when I share this work I do, the struggles I have, the real grit of this life and, ultimately, the knowledge that I choose how I show up.

That is how I knew that coaching, supporting, holding space for, and encouraging other women to do the same was my calling.

It is a beautiful marriage of strategy and learning with alignment of our thoughts and choices. I call it fierce and flowy.

Each day, I connect with, teach, share, and offer this energy to the world in the form of inspiration, masterclasses, programs, coaching, mentorship, and hypnotherapy. I show up. And when my clients do too, they feel the shifts within.

That's what makes the most difference in the lives of the women I support. That they show up for themselves. Unapologetically. Taking even five minutes of time each day to pause, breathe, reflect. To do the work from the inside out.

My best work happens when I tune in and listen to the inspiration within. This is when I feel most aligned. It is non-negotiable that I take this time so I can continue to create content, classes, and training that support women from all walks of life to amplify their energy, influence, and income in this big, beautiful world.

When you take these steps, anything is possible.

It's time to find your heaven on earth.

To receive the words 'You are the gift.'

This truth is most certainly all around you, patiently waiting for you to access it.

***

To connect with Helen:

Connect with Helen on Facebook, LinkedIn, Instagram, YouTube @Helen Eimers or visit www.heleneimers.com to book a discovery call to learn how you can find support with a beautiful collaboration of strategy and mindset work so you too can open your heart to bigger shifts and endless possibilities that await you in this beautiful life.

www.heleneimers.com

Facebook @helen.eimers

Instagram @heleneimers

Facebook Group: Midlife Womenpreneur Success Community

Ryan Herpin

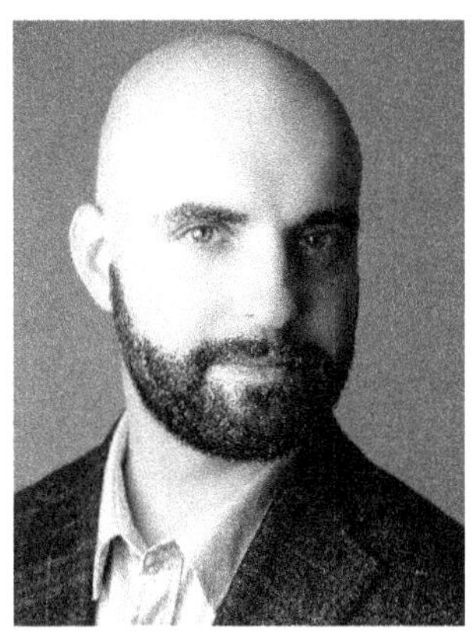

Ryan Herpin, born on October 22, 1996, in Battle Creek, Michigan, is the son of Sarah Downs and Roy Herpin Jr. Raised in a large family with five brothers and one sister, Ryan's work ethic and determination were instilled early. He launched his career as a Certified Welding Technician, where he honed his technical skills and quickly advanced in the manufacturing industry. His expertise and leadership led him to the role of Director of Operations for a major manufacturing company.

In this position, Ryan played a pivotal role in transforming the company's fortunes, guiding it from struggling to maintain profitability to an impressive sale at 33 times EBITDA in just four years. Inspired by this success, Ryan pursued his entrepreneurial ambitions and founded Impact Strategies Consulting LLC. Through his firm, Ryan leverages his extensive experience and proven strategies to help businesses across a multitude of industries grow their profitability and achieve their full potential. His journey from a hands-on technician to a visionary business consultant exemplifies his dedication to excellence and his passion for helping others succeed.

From the Shop Floor to the Boardroom: Three Principles to My Success

By: Ryan Herpin

Success is often viewed as something reserved for those with privileged backgrounds or advanced degrees, but my journey has taught me that the true principles of success lie elsewhere. I was born into a lower-class family, surrounded by hard work and modest means. College wasn't a part of my story, and the world of academia was something I observed from the sidelines. Instead, I walked a different path, one forged in the heat of a welding shop, where hard work, sweat, big dreams, and a belief that someday I would be important were my guides.

Starting my journey as a welding technician, I was determined to rise above my circumstances. Despite the challenges I faced, I knew that I had the power to shape my own future. My journey wasn't defined by the lack of formal education but by the consistent self-discipline I applied to master my skills. My purpose—my "why"—fueled my persistence, pushing me to keep going even when the road seemed impossibly tough.

However, I didn't walk this path alone. Along the way, I was fortunate to surround myself with people who believed in me even when I had moments of doubt. Friends, mentors, and colleagues who saw potential in me provided guidance, encouragement, and sometimes a much-needed push. They didn't just support me; they fueled my ambitions, helping me to see beyond the limits of my upbringing. Their belief in my potential often served as a mirror, reflecting the possibilities that I sometimes struggled to see in myself. Through these relationships, I learned the importance of surrounding yourself with those who lift you up, challenge you, and push you to strive for more.

This chapter delves into the very elements that propelled me forward: a powerful sense of purpose, unwavering self-discipline, and an unshakeable belief in myself—fueled by the support of those who walked alongside me. These are the pillars upon which I built my life, and they are the same principles that can transform anyone's journey, regardless of where they start. Applying these principles led me from welder to director to entrepreneur. Success is not just a destination; it's a process of continuous growth, guided by the values and beliefs we hold dear and strengthened by the people we choose to walk with. As you read on, I hope my story and the insights within will inspire you to harness these principles and create your path to success.

Purpose

From a young age, I knew I wanted to be successful, meaningful, and respected. I didn't just want to get by; I wanted to make a real impact on the world. Knowing you want these things and understanding why you want them are two very different things. Early in my career as a welder, I was driven by a hunger to prove myself, but I lacked a clear purpose behind that drive. I pushed forward because I wanted to become someone, but I hadn't yet discovered the deeper reason behind my ambitions.

It wasn't until I met Jack Smith, a mentor who would play a pivotal role in my journey, that I began to uncover my true purpose. Jack, the owner of the company I worked for, came into my life when the view of my path forward became difficult. He put me in a leadership role and saw something in me that I hadn't fully recognized in myself. He was the kind of mentor who didn't just guide; he challenged. Jack would often ask me, "Why do you want this? What's driving you?" At first, I struggled to answer. I knew I wanted success, but I couldn't articulate the deeper reasons why.

Jack's mentorship methods wouldn't have worked for everyone. It took grit to withstand the internal war he could inspire. Amid the many difficult questions, a few remain at the forefront of my mind, serving as a compass that continually guides me toward my true north. We as people struggle to comprehend death and what comes after. Most of us, including myself, would avoid the thought of our funeral, but Jack saw this as a path to discovering my why. He asked, "If you died right now, who would be at your funeral? What would they say about the life you lived? How would you be remembered?" The answer can easily be surface level, but the truth requires a deep dive into who you really are at the core. I took his guidance seriously and reflected on these questions. The truth was, I wasn't the person

I aspired to be, and I've hardly made a positive impact worth remembering. His follow-up questions led me to discover my purpose. "When you die, how do you want to be remembered? What do you want people to say about the life you lived? Who is the person that deserves to be remembered?" I encourage everyone to answer these questions, for they provided the push I needed to turn my dreams into reality.

Jack wasn't one to accept superficial answers. He pushed me, sometimes to the point of nearly breaking. He would make me question everything: my motivations, goals, and the core of who I was. It was uncomfortable, even painful at times, but it was necessary. Jack believed that without a clear purpose, all the success in the world would feel hollow. He challenged me to dig deeper, to go beyond the surface-level desires of fame or financial gain, and to discover the true reason behind my drive.

Through this process, I began to realize that my purpose was rooted in something much more profound than personal success. I wanted to make a difference, not just in my life but in the lives of others. I wanted to be a force for positive change, to use my skills and experiences to help others rise above their circumstances, just as I had. This understanding became the foundation of my purpose, guiding every decision and action I took from that point forward.

Discovering my "why" transformed my approach to everything. It gave me clarity, focus, and an unshakeable resolve to pursue my goals with renewed vigor. Purpose isn't just about what you want to achieve; it's about why you want to achieve it. Once you discover your why, it becomes the foundation upon which your success is built, and like the foundation of a building, while necessary to be laid first, it is not sufficient on its own.

Self-Discipline

When I first started as a welder, I quickly realized that talent alone wasn't enough to be counted among the six-figure technicians. It was the consistent self-discipline I applied to mastering every technique and every detail that set me apart. Welding requires precision, patience, and a relentless commitment to improvement. I spent countless hours honing my skills, practicing even the smallest tasks until they became second nature. This wasn't easy; there were days

I wanted to cut corners or take the easy way out, but I knew that doing so would only cheat me out of the excellence I was striving for.

The same self-discipline that drove me to master welding became the vehicle for my growth as a leader. As I transitioned into management roles, I quickly realized that leading a team required just as much, if not more, discipline. It wasn't enough to simply give orders; I had to lead by example, maintain a strong work ethic, and continuously develop my leadership abilities. Just as I had with welding, I dedicated myself to learning everything I could about leadership—reading books, seeking advice from experienced leaders, and reflecting on my own experiences.

Consistency was key. Every day, I made a conscious effort to improve, whether it was in how I communicated with my team, handled challenges, or made decisions. I approached leadership with the same meticulous attention to detail that I had applied to welding. Over time, this discipline paid off. I began to see the results not just in my own growth but in the success of the teams I led. My dedication to constant improvement fostered a culture of excellence, where every team member was encouraged to push their limits and strive for greatness.

However, the benefits of self-discipline extend far beyond career performance. Consistent self-discipline has a powerful impact on you as a person. It builds resilience, strengthens your character, and reinforces your sense of self-worth. When you commit to disciplined actions, you gain a sense of control over your life. You become someone who can be relied upon, not just by others but by yourself. This reliability fosters confidence, enabling you to tackle challenges with a calm and focused mindset.

Self-discipline also cultivates patience and long-term thinking. In a world where instant gratification is the norm, the ability to delay rewards and stay focused on your long-term goals is a rare and valuable trait. It teaches you to appreciate the process and to find satisfaction in the incremental progress that ultimately leads to significant achievements. This mindset is crucial for turning dreams into reality. Big dreams require consistent effort over time, and self-discipline ensures you keep moving forward, even when progress seems slow, or obstacles appear insurmountable.

Self-discipline is, at its core, the engine for building success; the steady, relentless force compels us to persevere, push forward, and continually strive for improvement. It's what turns aspirations into actions and actions into achievements. In my journey, self-discipline was the bridge between mastering a technical skill and becoming an effective leader, but it was also the force that shaped me into the person I am today. It has not only fueled my professional growth but has formed me into a husband and father who leads by example.

Applying consistent self-discipline to the pursuit of fulfilling your purpose is one of the most powerful decisions you can make in life. When you commit yourself fully to your purpose and approach it with unwavering discipline, the rewards that follow are often immeasurable and far beyond what you initially imagined. This is because true success comes not just from achieving specific goals but from the growth, fulfillment, and inner peace that arise from living in alignment with your purpose.

It's important to understand that this process isn't about chasing after rewards or recognition. Instead, it's about dedicating yourself to your purpose with pure intent—to give your best, to make a difference, and to fulfill your potential. When you focus on the work itself, being the best you can be, and contributing to something greater than yourself, the rewards come naturally and often unexpectedly. These rewards are a byproduct of genuine effort and passion, not the primary motivation. By shifting your focus from outcomes to impact, you allow success to flow to you organically.

The beauty of this approach is that it allows you to find joy and fulfillment in the journey, not just the destination. When you push forward without expecting, you free yourself from the pressure of external validation and the fear of failure. Your motivation comes from your purpose and is sustained by your self-discipline. As you continue giving your all, the rewards will follow, not because you demanded them but because they are the natural result of living purposefully and disciplined. This creates a cycle of fulfillment and success, where your commitment to your purpose continually draws more opportunities and rewards into your life.

Unshakable Belief

Self-belief wasn't merely a choice; it was an absolute necessity. Early in my career, as I transitioned from a welder to a leadership role, there were countless moments where self-doubt could have easily derailed my progress. I was stepping into unfamiliar territory, taking on responsibilities I had never imagined myself handling. In those moments, the only thing that kept me moving forward was an unshakable belief in my ability to figure it out, to rise to the challenge, and to ultimately find a way.

A strong belief in myself was critical for sticking to my purpose. When you believe in yourself, you give yourself permission to dream big and pursue goals that might seem impossible to others. Self-belief holds you tightly to your purpose because it allows you to see beyond your current circumstances and imagine what could be. My belief kept me focused on my purpose—to make a significant impact not just in my own life but in the lives of others. It strengthened my desire to keep pushing, even when the path was unclear or difficult.

Belief is critical for consistent self-discipline. Discipline requires you to do the hard things, to stay committed even when motivation is low, and to keep going in the face of setbacks. Without a strong belief in myself, it would have been easy to give up, to convince myself that the challenges were too great or that I wasn't capable of achieving what I set out to do. But because I believed in my ability to grow, learn, and overcome obstacles, I was able to maintain the discipline necessary to pursue my goals relentlessly.

Surrounding myself with people who fueled my ambition and reminded me of my purpose was equally paramount to my success. Throughout my journey, I was fortunate to have mentors, friends, and colleagues who believed in me just as much as I believed in myself. They saw my potential, even in moments when I struggled to see it. Their encouragement, advice, and sometimes tough love kept me grounded and focused on my goals. They reminded me of the bigger picture, the purpose behind my hard work, and the fact that I could achieve far more than I sometimes give myself credit for.

This network of support was invaluable, but it also reinforced the importance of choosing the right people to have in your corner. The people you surround yourself with can either build you up or tear you down. When you're surrounded by those who believe in you, who share your vision and encourage you to keep going, their faith in you makes your belief unshakeable. It's like having a safety net that catches you when you falter and pushes you back on track.

An unshakable belief in yourself acts as the glue that holds discipline tightly to purpose. It's what allows you to take risks and pursue dreams that others might dismiss as too ambitious. Without this belief, it's easy to lose sight of your goals or to be swayed by the opinions and doubts of others. But with it, you become unstoppable, capable of achieving far more than you ever thought possible.

Conclusion

Purpose, self-discipline, and unshakable belief—these three principles of success have been the driving forces behind every achievement in my life. They've guided me from the welding floor to the boardroom, from a young man with big dreams to the founder of a consulting firm that's making a real impact. These principles aren't just concepts but powerful tools that can take anyone to heights they never thought possible.

Developing a clear purpose gives you direction and a strong foundation on which to stand. It's the "why" behind everything you do, the reason you get up in the morning and push through challenges. When you have a strong purpose, it becomes the compass that guides your decisions and actions, ensuring that you stay on course even when the path is difficult.

Self-discipline is the engine that drives you forward. It's the commitment to consistent effort, even when motivation wanes or obstacles arise. With self-discipline, you build the habits and resilience needed to turn your purpose into reality. It's the daily dedication that transforms dreams into tangible success.

Unshakable belief is the glue that holds it all together. Believing in yourself and your abilities gives you the confidence to take risks and pursue your goals with passion and persistence. It's what keeps you going when others might give up, and it attracts opportunities and success into your life.

Through my consulting firm, I've had the privilege of helping others develop these three principles in their own lives. I've seen firsthand how, when aligned, these principles can elevate anyone to heights unknown, unlocking potential that even they didn't know they had. By helping others find their purpose, cultivate self-discipline, and build unshakable belief, I've found how to serve my purpose and obtain a flow of fulfillment.

These principles of success are universal. They're not reserved for the privileged or the lucky; they're available to anyone willing to put in the work. Whether you're just starting out or looking to take your life to the next level, focusing on these principles can propel you toward achievements you never imagined. With purpose, self-discipline, and unshakable belief, there are no limits to what you can achieve. This is the message I hope to leave with every person I work with: success isn't a destination; it's a journey of becoming the best version of yourself. And it's a journey that can take you as far as you're willing to go.

This is the legacy I strive to build—a legacy where the lessons of the three principles of success continue to inspire and empower others long after I'm gone. Every step I've taken has led me to this point, and through my consulting firm, I'm committed to helping others take their own steps toward a future where their dreams are not just possibilities but realities.

***

To contact Ryan:

Website: www.impactstrategiesc.com

Email: r.herpin@impactstrategiesc.com

LinkedIn: www.linkedin.com/in/ryan-herpin

Stephanie Brandolini

Stephanie Brandolini is a best-selling author, award-winning screenwriter, filmmaker, speaker and high-ticket business coach from Vancouver, British Columbia, Canada.

After graduating from film school, Stephanie worked her way up in the visual effects production world, gaining in-depth knowledge of the TV and film industry. Through her success and spirituality, Stephanie discovered a deeper calling to go all in on her writing and creative gifts and serve others.

Now, as a creative entrepreneur, she is on a mission to help driven individuals and families break free from the matrix, uplevel their health and finances, get their time back, and build a legacy. All while creating and collaborating on writing, film, and speaking projects that uplift, inspire and transform audiences worldwide.

From Weakness to Warrior: Rise Fearless, Claim Your Legacy

By Stephanie Brandolini

Face your fears—everything you want is on the other side of them...

Right?

Yes, but what does that really mean?

And what does it mean to truly be fearless?

Hello, dear reader, and welcome. Since you're reading this book, I imagine you've heard varieties of this motivational advice—to face, embrace, and heal your fears.

Let's be real, we all know fear holds us back, but breaking through it often feels elusive. We get amped up with motivation, ready to "just do it," but so many end up falling back into the same patterns of fear. The fire fades, and you're left feeling stuck, wondering why you can't seem to break free.

Why do we fall back into fear?

It's easy to blame ourselves, to think we're somehow broken or that "this is just the way I am."

But is that really true?

Fear is a part of human nature, yes. It's there to keep us safe, to protect us from danger. But what happens when fear becomes our prison? When it holds us back from the life we're meant to live?

Before we go further I must ask you a very important question:

Would you rather stay at the human level…

Or go supernatural?

Since you're still with me, I commend you. You're one of the brave ones. Going supernatural isn't just a want; it's a calling. And if you feel that call, then keep reading, because by the end of this chapter, you'll never look at fear the same way again.

What Lies Beneath?

Before we go deeper, let me introduce myself properly so we're not total strangers. As my bio mentioned, my name is Stephanie, I'm a creative entrepreneur, and on my journey, I didn't just discover who I am—I discovered whose I am.

More on that later.

For now, just know that I'm no one special, but I am someone who said yes to my dreams, yes to evolving, and yes to my highest life.

But I wasn't always such a yes woman.

In fact, I was once so driven by fear I couldn't even see how lost and trapped I truly was. For fifteen years, I was trapped in the grips of a severe eating disorder—an illness that nearly took my life. Fear developed the disorder, and through faith, I eventually broke free.

It wasn't just about beating the disorder; it was about confronting the deep-seated fears that I had buried beneath it. My recovery became a mission of dismantling these layers of fear and overcoming each one, step by step.

From this an even greater mission was unearthed: to show others that they can break free and create a better life out of the ashes of who they once were.

Our struggles, our trials, and how we overcome are woven into the grand tapestry of who we are, but that doesn't mean we need to stay stuck in them—especially if they're no longer serving us.

Facing the Darkness Within

When faced with dysfunctional behaviors or recurring challenges, most people's instinct is to avoid them, but avoidance keeps you stuck.

So, instead of running, I invite you to pause, hold space for your struggles, and face them head-on!

That's the first step: facing and accepting.

It likely won't be easy, especially at first. But with repetitive acceptance of the fact that you are, in fact, choosing those behaviors, you'll begin to rewire your mind away from those patterns. And with every step of awareness and acceptance, you're forging new, healthier neural pathways.

Here's something essential to remember during this phase: don't let guilt, shame, or any self-critical thoughts get to you. Those are your ego's tricks, trying to pull you back into the very patterns you need to break free from. The ego loves to cling to fear, and the enemy loves to use our ego against us to keep us from rising into our God-given dreams. More to come on that shortly, but at this point in our journey together, know that you've got to feel the uncomfortableness of accepting that you've been stuck because of x, y, and z so you can let them go and move forward.

I get it though, it's tempting to think, "Why did I let myself stay stuck for so long?" or "How could I have been so weak?" But those thoughts will only sabotage your progress. That's not you speaking—that's fear trying to take over again. This is where you get to choose to recognize those thoughts for what they are: distractions that lead to destruction.

You're not defined by your fears or failures. You're defined by what you choose to do next and how you let go of the lack that's holding you back along the way.

Letting Go… Or Something More?

Ah, letting go, every guru's favourite phrase, am I right? It's everywhere, in every self-help book, on every motivational podcast. But what does that really mean? And how do you actually do it?

Well, first off, it's not exactly something you do; it's something you be.

Letting go is a simple concept, but simple doesn't mean easy. Especially if you've been living in fear for years, letting go can feel impossible.

But guess what?

Faith feeds on the impossible.

And in faith, there's something even more powerful than letting go…

Your choice to *surrender*.

Surrender is another one of those terms that gets thrown around in the personal development world, but not all surrender is created equal.

I personally found my healing in surrendering to God through Jesus Christ—which was honestly a surprise to me at first. Christianity used to feel very imposing, rule bound, and just not for me. Plus, there are Christian sects that I definitely don't agree with or condone the behavior of.

But what I found in my surrender wasn't any kind of religion. Instead, it was an all-encompassing, unconditional love, and a supreme peace that surpasses all understanding. That peace led to enigmatic empowerment, allowing me to develop a personal relationship to divinity on my own terms.

And here's the thing, when it comes to God, there's no condemnation, only love. It really is that simple, but we overcomplicate it. As much love that's come through faith, that very faith can get warped and twisted into zealotry, anger, and destruction.

The very opposite of the intention!

Oh, the bitter irony, eh?

I get it though; I was once there in my own way.

There were days in my past when I'd yell at God, demanding to know just why the fuck I was here and what the point was when I was in so much misery—but even then, I tacked onto that prayer:

"If you can promise me, God, that one day I'll know what it means to be truly happy, then let me live."

He did, and I do, and I am forever grateful.

But happiness didn't come for me in the snap of God's fingers. It came in healing the layers of myself that were blocking my true potential.

The catalyst to my healing came when God saved my life. I was at death's door due to the eating disorder I'd mentioned previously. To paint a not-so-beautiful picture, I'm five-foot seven inches tall and weighed a measly 89 pounds—and trust me, I did not look good. I knew it too, but I couldn't help the perverse desire to see those numbers on the scale keep going down, and down, and down.

During this dark night of my soul, many years ago, having no knowledge of scripture, divine healing, or really any kind of healthy connection with God; when I was about to fall asleep one night, I faced a fear I didn't expect to even care about—the fear that I might not wake up the next day.

I could feel my dying heart beating, but I knew it couldn't keep it up. Not with what I was doing to myself—and at that point it wasn't even really me—the disorder had taken on a life of its own. I'd always imagined it as a femme fatale frenemy, but now, I know it was the enemy: the devil himself trying to take me out.

That fateful night, I rose from my bed and stepped shakily downstairs to my family's library and pulled out The Holy Bible. I clutched it to my chest as I fell asleep, somehow reciting Psalm 23 even though I'd never actually read it…

Though I walk through the valley of the shadow of death I will fear no evil, for thou art with me.

God was with me that night. He'd been there all along, and He answered my spirit's cry through my mum calling an ambulance and having me taken to the hospital against my will.

It wasn't my will that I'm still here, it was God's.

He saved me for a time such as this.

This divine intervention was a seed planted that came to harvest as I stepped into entrepreneurship.

Now I know my life was saved so I can help others choose to change their lives and claim their God-given dreams.

But the not so silent killer to divine dreams is…

You guessed it, fear.

Transmuting Weakness into Strength

Fear breeds insecurities, which we come to think of as weaknesses. I once thought my eating disorder was my greatest weakness. I believed it was something broken inside me, something that I would never overcome.

But here's what revelation brought me: the disorder wasn't just a health issue. It was a symptom of deeper fears, insecurities, and lies I had believed about myself. The disorder was a mask I wore to hide the real problem: fear.

Fear of not being enough. Fear of not being loved. Fear of failure.

And here's what changed everything for me: when I surrendered in faith, those fears weren't just removed, they were transmuted by God.

Notice a key shift here—God did the work. My work lay in receiving this blessing He'd been trying to give me all along.

That's the thing about God, He doesn't force anything on you. He's a gentleman who knows what's best for you, but it's always a two-way street. If you choose God, He will take what you thought was your greatest flaw, your greatest burden, and turn it into your greatest strength with the might of His eternal light.

The one light to rule them all.

When I surrendered not just my eating disorder, but all the bullshit the disorder was covering up, God showed me that the very thing that had been holding me back for so long could become my greatest testimony. He turned my weakness into a source of strength—not just for myself, but for others.

The purpose of sharing my testimony here is for you, dear reader, to know that whatever you're struggling with, whatever weakness you think you have, it can be transformed into something greater than you ever imagined when you surrender it in faith to God.

That's where your weakness ends, His strength takes over, and you become a fearless warrior.

Now this is when something incredible happens: you awaken to what you're truly here for.

Your potential may have been blocked by fear, but when fear is transformed, that potential starts to rise. It starts to take form. And it's not just potential anymore—it's purpose.

Your purpose isn't something you just discover one day out of the blue. It's something that's been inside you all along, like a seed that's been planted in your spirit, waiting for the right conditions to grow.

When you face your fears, surrender your weaknesses, and walk in faith, you create the atmosphere for that seed to bloom and your purpose ignites! Then you realize it's not just about you.

Your purpose is bigger than you.

It's about the impact you're meant to have on the world, the people you're here to serve, the lives you're meant to change, the difference you're destined to make.

Quantum Shifts & Spiritual Law

Here's the incredible thing about this process: it doesn't have to take long. It can, if you believe it does—but it doesn't have to. With consistent practice and faith in your best possible outcome, you can experience quantum shifts. These are rapid, almost instantaneous shifts in mindset and circumstances that can happen when you align your thoughts with the power of faith and the abundance that's always been available to you.

This shift applies to all areas of life—relationships, health, personal fulfillment, wealth. Abundance is everywhere when you learn how to see it. The more you focus on what you have, the more you will receive.

This is a spiritual law: what you focus on expands.

So, if you feel lack in one area of your life, focus on the abundance you already have in another. Let that abundance expand and grow like a muscle and ripple out into the areas where you feel scarcity. As you keep building your abundance muscle, you'll see how lack transforms into more than enough. Shifting into an abundance mindset in this way combines rewiring your mind and aligning with a deeper spiritual truth.

God declares, "So is my word that goes out from my mouth: It will not return to me empty but will accomplish what I desire and achieve the purpose for which I sent it." - Isaiah 55:11

God's word never returns void, my friend. What He speaks is guaranteed to come to pass.

If you believe in His word and act on it, you activate the power of spiritual law. It's not just about thinking positively or visualizing abundance—it's about having unshakeable faith that God's promises will be fulfilled as you go forth, step by step. When you shift your mindset into alignment with divine abundance, you're allying yourself with the very laws of the universe that God created.

And from this faith-fueled foundation anything is possible.

And then…?

When you've walked the path from weakness to warrior, you're ready for the next level:

Legacy.

Legacy is about more than what you leave behind. It's about how you live your life daily. It's about the decisions you make, the values you hold, the impact you have on others, and the ripple effect your actions create.

Your legacy doesn't begin when you've reached some final level of success or when you've achieved all your goals. No. Your legacy is being built right now, in this moment, with every choice you make. You are living your legacy in the way you show up for others, in the way you walk through your challenges, and in the way you overcome your fears.

When you rise as a warrior—when you live fearlessly with purpose, strength, and intention—you don't just create a legacy.

You become the legacy.

Imagine what the world would look like if every person fully stepped into this way of being. Imagine the collective impact we'd have if each of us embraced our fears, surrendered them to God, and awakened to our divine purpose.

Imagine that butterfly ripple effect…

This kind of legacy doesn't happen by accident. It's a choice. It's something to be intentional about. You get to decide, every day, to live in a way that aligns with the values you uphold and impact you're called to create.

Maybe your legacy is tied to your family, your career, your creativity, your faith…

Whatever your legacy is, know this: it will require ongoing commitment. It will require courage. And most importantly, it will require you to keep showing up as the fearless warrior you've become.

Legacy is not about perfection. You don't have to wait until you've got everything figured out, or until you feel "ready," to be your legacy. You are already building it with every choice you make and the everyday decisions that reflect who you are and what you stand for.

Your legacy is also built in how you handle setbacks. Being a warrior doesn't mean you won't face obstacles. It means that when you do, you rise again and again.

You keep going. You persevere. That's the kind of legacy that lasts.

So, as we conclude, take a moment to reflect on the journey we've gone through together. I've shared how to face your fears, how to surrender them, how to transmute weakness into strength, and how to awaken to your purpose.

Now, it's time to ask yourself: what kind of legacy do you want to leave behind?

What do you want your life to stand for?

How do you want to be remembered?

And most importantly, WHY?

Don't forget that God is with you, if you choose Him to be. He has already equipped you with everything you need to succeed. The seeds of greatness live within you. All you have to do is trust God, follow His guidance, and take the next step believing it's all going to work out.

Your Calling

You've made it this far, and I want to congratulate you. You've taken the first steps toward something greater than you ever imagined. But the journey doesn't end here.

Now the real adventure begins. This is your call to greatness. This is your time to rise as a fearless warrior and create a legacy that shines long after you've left this earth.

Remember…

You are stronger than your fears.

You are greater than your doubts.

And with God by your side, there is nothing you can't overcome.

So, I ask you:

Are you ready to become fearless?

Are you ready to live your purpose, claim your abundance, be your legacy, and change the world?

The choice is yours.

If that choice is a heck yes! Let's connect on making it happen!

To contact Stephanie:

***

www.stephaniebrandolini.com

https://www.facebook.com/sbrandolini

https://www.instagram.com/stephbrandolini/

Steve Wormer

Steve Wormer is a proven leader who leads with integrity, strength and compassion. He has led a large district in a corporate company, a non-profit organization, and three churches. Following Jesus drives everything that he does.

Steve is trained in helping folks follow proven steps to help them with unprocessed emotions, such as unforgiveness, bitterness, anxiety, relationship challenges, etc.

Steve is a John Maxwell-certified speaker, coach, and trainer. He loves to share his powerful personal story from the stage, along with his eight steps to helping others get unstuck and take their next steps towards achieving their dreams.

Steve has been married to his lovely wife Rebecca for 28 years, and they have three wonderful kids.

Steve loves sports, working out, reading, and family vacations, especially ones that include the water.

Steve speaks on resiliency, leadership development, personal growth and development, and emotional intelligence.

The Change
Bridging The Gap: Moving From Trials to Breakthroughs

By Steve Wormer

Trials are hard, aren't they? I mean, they wouldn't be called trials if they were easy. I have observed that most people I know simply white knuckle their way out of their trails and cannot wait for it to be over so they can move on to better days. I am certainly not judging that in any way because I have also fit into that category for most of my life. I simply viewed trials as terrible, and that certainly wasn't fair. Can anyone relate?

As you have already experienced in your own life, you know that trials don't last forever. I want to remind you that there is always hope and that the breakthrough you seek is likely just around the corner! There is a breakthrough on the other side of your trial. We just must bridge the gap. We all want to move from the trial side of the bridge to the other side, where the breakthroughs are.

Have there been times when you were going through a trial, and you felt totally weary? How about frustrated? Or what about this one? Did you feel like your hope was wavering? Did you feel like your dreams were on the back burner during this trial? Did you feel like giving up? Did you feel like it just wasn't going to be worth pursuing your dreams because the trail to reaching it was just too hard?

Sometimes, it feels like we are like a car stuck on ice, trying to get out to a more stable land, but the tires keep spinning.

Has your hope ever waivered?

I know you have some dreams you want to see fulfilled. You are wired for dreams. We all have them. What goals do you have to reach those dreams? You've been hurt. You are tired. You have failed a time or two. You wonder what the point is. You wonder how much you have left to give. Silently, you have picked up the towel to give up on the dream you have in your heart.

I can relate to you. In fact, I have been in situations where my hope didn't just waver; my hope was life support. That is what happens sometimes when we go through trials.

My wife and experienced five miscarriages in six years. This was gut-wrenching to go through as a couple. I was young and did not know how to process my emotions personally, let alone help Rebecca through hers.

I remember how excited we were when she got pregnant for the first time. Of course, as a proud, soon-to-be father, I told everyone who would listen. Of course, I told family and close friends. I told my co-workers and neighbors. Goodness, I told the cashier at the grocery store!

I remember having Nextel cell phones for my job at the time. Remember the Nextel phones? They were part phone and part walkie-talkie. It was a great concept, but not so much functionality!

After the first couple of miscarriages, I got tired of telling my family and friends that we were pregnant again. And we eventually had five miscarriages in six years.

I got weary of getting all excited just to have my hopes dashed. Forget about me, however. What about my wife?

To be honest, it hurt me. I was young, focused on work, and emotionally immature. The truth is I didn't think nearly enough about what my wife was going through. I mean, let's be honest. It stank for both of us, but she had the rough end of this situation.

Obviously, it was not because I didn't care about her or what she was going through. I just couldn't do anything to fix it.

I am not the guy who fixes things around the house, but many of you are. Man, I respect your skills.

But in general, we guys are "get it done" types. "Let's fix this issue." I am a helper. A servant. But my wife was hurting. She had lost six babies. I got nothing. I couldn't fix that one. It was above my pay grade.

Hope doesn't just waver; it goes on life support when we can't fix it.

My wife and I started discussing adoption. Processing together, praying together, and discussing it with close friends. We were really considering the idea of growing our family through adoption.

We went through the entire process: we selected an adoption agency, we went through the scheduled training courses, we had pictures taken of us and our dogs, and we had our home inspected.

We were selected quickly by a birthmother who was seven months pregnant and who lived about an hour away.

We got close to the birthmother and her family. We truly all had a bond and got along well.

My wife went to all the remaining doctor's appointments with her.

She let us give the unborn girl her name.

As you can imagine, we were so excited! We had been waiting so long—so many years.

Buying the baby clothes, crib, diapers, and formula, and getting the baby's room ready for her arrival.

Some close friends even threw Rebecca a baby shower.

Target and Walmart were going to see us more frequently, for sure.

Now came the time for the birthmother to check into the local hospital.

We were there for the entire weekend.

We had already named the baby Hope, as the birthmother permitted us to name the child.

It was a glorious day and moment when Hope entered the world. Our dreams were coming true.

Rebecca was in the delivery room when Hope was born. The nurses immediately came to get me and took me to a private waiting room close by. I came in, and the baby was handed to me. I had never held a newborn before. Babies, yes. A baby literally that just arrived here on earth, nope; I had not experienced that before. I noticed the delivery room resembled a war zone! Man! But mostly, I remember the proud feeling of holding my baby girl.

Then it happened.

What is it?

The birthmother changed her mind on Sunday morning, right before we were supposed to leave the hospital with our child.

We went home empty-handed but learned a lot about forgiveness, contentment, surrender, and compassion during this time.

We went on to have another failed adoption. And another. And another. And another. And another. And one more!

We lived through six failed adoptions in what had become an almost five-year adoption journey. Our hope wavered.

Have you ever felt that way? Ever felt that your passion, your zeal, your hope was wavering?

What we needed at that time was a massive shot of hope. We needed a breakthrough.

You see, the hope of a breakthrough sustains a person. It keeps them going when times are tough. Sometimes, it may just be a flicker of hope, but that flicker is enough.

Does anyone here need less hope? I have yet to find a person who needs less of the stuff. What qualifies me to speak on such an essential topic as hope? Good question. I can only speak from personal experience. I have been in several situations and put myself in several situations that required hope for me to get unstuck from whatever held me back at the time.

The hope of a breakthrough is a way of thinking that involves future-oriented optimism. It's a pervasive, positive outlook that the pathways to your desired goals exist and are achievable, even in the face of extreme challenges.

Hope gives us the nudge to persist when we want to stay in our heads or in our beds.

A 2020 longitudinal study from the Psych Central website (www.psychcentral.com) concluded that a survey of nearly 13,000 people found a greater sense of hope was associated with:

Reduced all-cause morality

Fewer chronic health conditions

Lower risk of cancer

Fewer sleep challenges

Increased positive mindset

Better life satisfaction

Maintaining a sense of purpose in life

Lower psychological distress

Better social well-being

8 Steps to Gain Momentum:

Here are 8 steps that I have developed to help you gain momentum.

These steps will help bridge the gap between your trails and your much-needed breakthroughs.

Step 1: Choose Gratitude

Like most things in my life, it has taken me a long time to learn valuable lessons. Gratitude is vital!

I remember a time when I lost my job in my early 30s. It was a good job. I made a good salary, had good benefits, a company car, and regularly got a quarterly bonus.

I lost it all. Most of it was not my fault, but that was not the point.

I was out of work for about six months. Sure, I had interviews, but I wasn't getting decent offers.

I interviewed with a non-profit organization, and the interview went well. I did not get the position I interviewed for. I must have made a decent impression, as they called me back a couple of weeks later to see if I would be interested in interviewing for another position. I did, and I ended up getting that position. Yes, employed once again!

Here is the thing, however. On my first day on the job, they had me reading client files—all day long! I was typically the decision maker, a mover and a shaker. Now, I was bored out of my mind. So much so that during my first break, maybe 2-3 hours into the first workday, I went to the back parking lot and called my recruiter and specifically told her, "You got to get me out of here!"

I was so ungrateful. Yes, the job wasn't my dream job, but I needed to give it a chance. We had bills to pay. I know Rebecca was grateful that at least now I would have some steady income. I ended up at that organization for 12 years. During those 12 years, I learned so many valuable life and professional lessons.

Gratitude is vital, friends.

Grateful is a beautiful place to be. I have found that gratitude is the great equalizer to many of the negative mindsets I can have. Gratitude gives me the right mindset when my circumstances are less than ideal.

It is nearly impossible to be grateful and worried at the same time. One will push the other away. So, we have a choice to make. Will we choose gratitude or something else?

Having a heart of gratitude helped sustain me through some of the heaviest trails of my life.

Gratitude is cumulative. It grows. As I sow gratitude, my joy increases as well. The more specific we get with our gratitude; our joy will be more effective. Gratitude eventually will become a feeling. We reap what we sow. So, my emotions will reflect what I am thinking about.

Your Circle Matters

Your trial feels overwhelming when you don't have a healthy support circle.

Do you have a support network? What does that circle look like? They should be supportive, encouraging, and challenging you at times. You should trust them with your dreams. They should hold you accountable for the action steps you have communicated with them that you want to take toward your dreams.

They should be there to help you when you fail and to encourage you when you hit the road bumps that we all hit on the road to eventual success.

We don't have time to discuss all the different types of healthy relationships that you could have in your circle, but we can quickly name a few.

Best friend

Mentor

Advisor

Coach

Accountability Partner

Counselor if needed

Then there is the support team. Depending on your goals, you may need a grant writer, a publisher, an editor, a graphic designer, a social media content person, or a virtual assistant. This list could continue, but I just want you to see that you need quality people around you.

You might be able to go fast by yourself, but you will go further with a team.

Self-Care Is Not Selfish

When you neglect self-care, your trial can feel overwhelming.

It is easy when you are stuck and start neglecting yourself. It is far too easy to pick up unhealthy eating habits. It's easy not to get the sleep your body and mind need. It can be far too easy to isolate yourself. Many, when stuck, aren't open to what they are feeling. Eat, rest, talk, walk, go to the gym, read a book, etc. Do something consistently that energizes you and gives you peace.

Are you getting 7-8 hours of sleep a night? Do you have a nighttime routine that helps you get the quality sleep you need?

Are you eating a healthy diet? This one is tough, especially when you are running wide open, and fast food is the convenient selection. Man, I love Mexican food. There is nothing like a good plate of nachos! However, I cannot make a habit of eating nachos four times a week and be pleased with the health goals I want to achieve.

When you make self-care a priority, you feel good about yourself. When you feel good about yourself – hope is alive.

Minimize Limiting Beliefs

Sometimes, we are our worst enemy by the way we think about ourselves. There are a variety of limited mindsets:

Imposter Syndrome

Frear of Success

Fear of Failure

Procrastination

Fixed Mindset

Self-Criticism

Blaming Others

Scripting Worse Case Scenarios

These are just a few. We all struggle with limited mindsets from time to time. The goal is to continue to grow and minimize these limited beliefs as they hinder our growth. Plenty of resources are out there to help us with our limiting beliefs.

Dump Excessive Baggage

All of us traveling on this journey on planet Earth collect emotional wounds and scars as we travel along the path set out for us. No one escapes without pain. Many are still carrying around that baggage. Unforgiveness, bitterness, anxiety, disappointments, addiction, relationship challenges, grief, the list goes on and on. Why do I bring this up here?

Because I want you to know that you are not alone; I want you to know that we all have stuff. I want you to know that these things no longer have to hold you back. I want you to know that there is hope.

I know that carrying unnecessary baggage from the past made this situation more difficult.

Professional therapists can help. There are also programs out there that can help minimize that excessive baggage you may have been carrying for way too long. The world needs the best version of you. Those close to you need the best version of you. Let's shed that excessive baggage and walk in freedom to be all that we can be to serve others. Let's be the best version of ourselves.

Get A Good Coach

I cannot even begin to tell you how much professional coaching has helped me grow as a leader. I have had one coach for over five years now, and I just recently started with a second coach. I am achieving my goals like never before.

I have two professional development coaches. They typically have me focused on some goals and dreams and then take action steps towards those goals. I have lots of notes and action steps and am excited to work on those in between sessions. Having the right coach can go a long way in helping you reach your dreams and bridging the gap between trials and breakthroughs.

Be An Avid Reader

"The more you read, the more things you will know. The more that you learn, the more places you'll go." - Dr. Seuss

I wasn't always an avid reader. I would read the occasional biography of one of my sports heroes, and that was about it. However, in the past 20 years, I have become a lover of reading. I love spiritual books, biographies, self-help books, and books on leadership.

I am fascinated by learning from a healthy variety of authors who share their wisdom with us in print. I love reading so much that just a few years ago, Rebecca made me quit buying hardcover and paperback books because they had filled a few bookcases, and we were running out of room to collect more.

I was hesitant to embrace technology at first and started buying Kindle books, but I love it! If I have my tablet with me, I have my books at my fingertips all the time.

Serve Someone

What you are going through is real. I don't want to minimize that. However, when we can help someone else, we become a blessing to the other person, obviously, but it is also beneficial for us. When we serve someone, we give the other person a little shot of hope.

It doesn't have to be a big project, either. You can drop someone off a meal, give them a ride somewhere, or run an errand for them.

When you think of someone else and do something to serve their needs, you will feel good about yourself.

In closing, I want to leave you with this: You are closer to your breakthrough than you may think. Take one step today, no matter how small that step may be.

Call on the Lord in your trials. He is listening. May His words to the prophet Jeremiah inspire you to start moving from one side of the bridge to the other. "Call to me and I will answer you and tell you great and unsearchable things you do not know."

I trust you will begin to see movement as you bridge the gap. You will indeed move from your trials to breakthroughs! And I, for one, cannot wait to hear all about it!

Quotes from Steve:

"Hope Is The Light At The End Of The Tunnel When You Were Sure It Was Another Train."

"Hope and Gratitude Are Siblings. They Work Together To Help You Ride Out The Storm To See Brighter Days."

"Hope Is The Fuel That Drives You Further Just When You Thought You Were Out Of Gas."

"Your Dream Is Huge! Never downsize your dream!"

***

https://stevewormer.com/

booknow@stevewormer.com

https://www.linkedin.com/in/steve-wormer-bb54b813/

https://www.facebook.com/steve.wormer/

https://www.youtube.com/@stevewormer5957

Kristi Mallory

Kristi Mallory is an executive coach with a leadership and organizational dynamics background. With nearly thirty years of experience, including a tenure as a VP in manufacturing, Kristi leverages her expertise to guide executives in leading with empathy, competence, and courage.

Her academic credentials include an MA in Organizational Leadership from the Townsend Institute at Concordia University in Irvine, CA. Kristi is also a certified coach with the International Coach Federation (ICF), known for her practical and authentic coaching style where she provides honest feedback and tangible results for leaders facing challenges.

Beyond coaching, Kristi is an adjunct professor at Concordia University, where she teaches graduate-level courses on organizational leadership and executive coaching. She is the creator of Momentum for Women, a Brené Brown certified Dare to Lead™ facilitator, and the author of *The Four Habits That Sabotage Exceptional Leaders*.

Kristi Mallory advocates for an integrated life, emphasizing the importance of balance and fulfillment beyond professional achievements. Her personal interests include fishing, art collecting, birdwatching, and spending quality time with her adult children. She splits her time between Tulsa and San Antonio, where she shares her home with her French Bulldog, Bailee.

Pinnacle Moments

By Kristi Mallory

He crossed the finish line in 26 hours and 46 minutes. All the blood, sweat, and tears over the past few months that led up to that instant made it worth the sacrifice. My son set out on a journey to run a hundred-mile race, and he did it.

The definition of "pinnacle" is the culmination and most successful point of a journey. To me, a pinnacle moment isn't just about reaching the peak of success; it's also the most transformative moments that shape our lives. When was your last pinnacle moment?

When Max crossed the finish line, I was overcome with emotion and pride, feeling deeply grateful and connected to his running community. I am not a runner, but I definitely experienced what could only be described as a runner's high as the culmination of 100 miles, 26+ hours of running, and the months of preparation ended. The experience embodied everything I believe in:

- Setting a goal.
- Taking small steps daily to achieve it.
- Receiving the unwavering support and accountability needed to see it through to the end.

Seeing my son complete this challenge was one of the most rewarding moments of my life.

Pinnacle moments don't just happen. They require a goal, an understanding of your intrinsic motivation, and a support system.

Not all goals end in a pinnacle moment, but BHAGs do. A BHAG is a big, hairy, audacious goal from the book Built to Last, written by Jim Collins. Daily goals are about taking small steps every day that will get you closer to your desired outcome. Stretch goals cause you to reach an ambitious objective. A BHAG will require both time and consistency. What was the last BHAG you set for yourself?

Cultivating intrinsic motivation is critically essential to discovering what drives you. Begin by identifying, understanding, and embracing personal values. Knowing your "why" will anchor your purpose, which opens the path to your authentic self. Once your values are discovered, you can authentically pursue mastery in your area of interest.

I am a firm believer in surrounding yourself with a team of people who will support you and hold you accountable. Max was surrounded by friends and family who did everything from providing water refills, fresh socks and food to "pacing" (running alongside). He was inspired to run 100 miles by his brother-in-law Angel, an avid runner and competitor. A sound support system includes ride-or-die people, coaches, trainers, and therapists. Don't do life without them.

What are the Roadblocks to Reaching Pinnacle Moments?

Roadblock One: Fierce Independence

Four common behaviors prevent people from attaining pinnacle moments. The first is being fiercely independent. Independence and autonomy are essential qualities. So, where is the line between healthy independence and fierce independence? Fierce independence occurs in the absence of collaboration. When an individual is detached or separated, that independence no longer serves the greater good.

I don't know of a single idea that doesn't benefit from another set of eyes and ears. Ideas become more concrete when they are challenged. The problem with being fiercely independent is being disconnected. When people operate in silos, they become separated from their peers. Consider the interdependent relationships of any ecosystem. It exists because of the interaction of all its parts. If one part isn't contributing, an imbalance occurs.

If you had to parent your parents or find you are driven by perfectionism, you may struggle with fierce independence. I get it. This might be a new concept for you. So many of us were taught not to be needy but instead to pull ourselves up by the bootstraps. Society has programmed us to believe that asking for help is a weakness. In some instances, growing up without deep relational connections has caused issues with being overly self-reliant. At times, people have been made to feel embarrassed or ashamed when asking for help.

The truth is humans are hard-wired to be connected with others. We are meant to need one another, and at the heart of needing each other is the truism of being needy.

This may come as a surprise, but every individual has needs. You are needy! YES, you are a needy person. The best way to meet your needs is to build a life team of safe people. Find individuals with whom you can mutually exchange thoughts, ideas, and feelings without being shamed, judged, or fixed.

If you identify with operating alone, I suggest you build a life team. Choose 3-7 people with whom you can share your thoughts and feelings. Test sharing your feelings and notice how they respond. You are looking for someone who can reciprocate by sharing their stories without hijacking the conversation, fixing it, and making it all about themselves.

Because most of us have been taught to fix things, often the conversation will need to start with, "I don't need any advice or fixing. I am just sharing". It is also worth mentioning that when building a life team, you can cultivate a diverse tribe you call on for one-to-one support.

When I first discovered this concept, I did not have a life team, and it took me a few years to build one. The most challenging part for me was finding local people. I had several people on my life team around the country, but finding people in my area added richness to my daily life. I treasure relationships with many peers, acquaintances, and friends, but finding life teamers requires deeper mutual sharing and trust. And that takes time.

Roadblock Two: Lack of Setting Limits

The second roadblock to reaching your pinnacle moments is a lack of setting limits. Many leaders today find themselves in a cycle of putting out fires with little time for anything else. Some have an open-door policy where the traffic flow is so heavy it keeps them from completing their daily tasks. Still, others are persuaded to sit in on meetings or take on extra job duties, leaving them no time to accomplish their to-do list. The issue is a lack of boundaries. The problem with not having limits is that you often feel out of control, overwhelmed, and have difficulty separating your needs from others.

The truth is that boundaries can be challenging to set and hard to keep, but they are one of the most vital skills to master. Developing the habit of setting boundaries is essential to how you connect and maintain separateness from those around you. Boundaries offer freedom. You know what you stand for and don't and can operate freely within those borders.

To master boundaries:

- Begin clearly understanding what's in your control.
- Determine what is yours to manage in any situation, relationship, or task, and stay in your lane.
- Resist the temptation to step in and pick up responsibilities that don't belong to you.

You always have a choice. Sometimes the only thing in your control is your response. Successful leaders know where to direct their energy and efforts to produce results.

When overwhelmed, it's time to take inventory of everything you're juggling. You may have accepted responsibility for duties that don't belong to you or taken on something outside of your authority. Prioritize and keep only those tasks that are under your control.

Get comfortable with saying no. No. No. No. No. No. Exercise that NO muscle! The more you flex your no, the easier it becomes. When you begin to say no, the opportunities to say yes begin to appear. The yes options become more apparent. Once you have carefully considered your choices and know what you want to say no to, then step into action. In this "yes and" culture, no is still relevant. Flex your no.

Encourage the practice of questioning, exploring, and disagreeing. Disagreement and conflict are a normal part of life. Instead of trying to win others over to your side, be curious and open to hearing what they say. Learn to respectfully state how your idea or opinion differs from someone else's. Validate others' ideas, even when you don't agree, or simply let them know you hear them. Being concise and direct is the kindest way to communicate.

Own your mistakes. It is human nature to blame someone else when things don't work. Blaming others or circumstances leaves people feeling helpless and like victims. Essentially, you give away your power. Taking ownership of your choices allows you to make corrections when necessary, rather than generate excuses that tend to keep you stuck.

When reflecting, take an honest look at your part in a conflict. Own your contribution. There should never be a time when you cannot find something that could be changed to yield a better outcome.

Setting limits is an acquired skill. The more you practice, the easier it becomes. Developing your boundary-setting muscles will significantly and positively impact your relationships.

Roadblock Three: How You Handle Negative Realities (aka Toxic Positivity)

A third roadblock to reaching a pinnacle goal is to minimize negative realities while putting a happy spin on everything. Toxic positivity is a common mindset issue. The problem is when you put a happy spin on a negative reality, important matters don't get solved. This habit can create a lack of trust. People can innately sense when something is wrong, and if told it's okay when it isn't, they will learn not to trust you. Possibly even worse than telling others it's okay when it's not, is telling yourself this.

We even see it in participation ribbons and the "everyone gets a trophy" philosophy in children's sports. Sometimes, you win, and sometimes, you lose. It's essential to learn how to do both. It becomes problematic when you minimize the truth, sweep things under the rug, or put lipstick on a pig to improve things. Negative realities don't just disappear because you spit-shine them.

I get it; it's very tempting to focus only on the positive, and maybe you are one of those leaders who really want to focus on others' strengths. Doing so only acknowledges half of the story. You can't understand the breadth and depth of an individual or issue if you are only observing one side.

When you dare to address negative situations, every voice gets a chance to be heard, opportunities for change are created, trust is built, and collaboration is welcomed because people feel safe to share.

When negative, undesirable, and challenging outcomes occur, they must be grieved. Grieving may take a minute, a month, or maybe a year or more. There is no limit on the amount of time it will take. When grief is present, you must have the courage to let people feel their feelings. Creating a safe space to acknowledge a loss will go a long way in developing trust and cohesiveness.

There are many things to consider when moving from toxic positivity to a reality-based perspective. Be aware when the tension of a difficult circumstance feels overwhelming to you. Upon closer examination, do you find your discomfort causes you to freeze and push you to move away from big feelings? Look out for anything holding you back from accepting the truth of a situation. These are signs you need to acknowledge a loss.

Grieving a loss can involve acknowledging the loss and its impact on you, allowing open conversations for others to share, and inviting acceptance without fixing. Once you've done these, you can move into fixing and repair. Don't dismiss or skip over grieving. It robs you of a growth opportunity.

The truth is that growth-minded people know how to face adverse outcomes and acknowledge their impact before moving forward. When things fall apart, look at negative realities as an opportunity for developing individual growth. Leaders don't lead because they know all the answers. Good leaders can admit they don't have the answer and then have the resolve to find the solution.

Creating space to grieve will build trust and credibility. The good news is you don't have to be perfect. What does need to happen is open, honest communication and acceptance of the situation.

Roadblock Four: Holding Reins Too Tightly (aka Micromanaging)

A fourth roadblock to reaching a pinnacle goal is how you present yourself in a relationship. Leadership today requires a consistent level of authority. Leaders who hold the reins too tightly appear to be micro-managers and exert power over their teams. Conversely, those who hold the reins too loosely present as having little power or an inability to lead effectively. Ideally, leaders should develop "power with" and "power to" posturing. This enables them to stand in their authority, inviting others to own their authority.

When a leader struggles with authority issues, the effects are severe and far-reaching. The problem is that they still need to identify and own their ideals and beliefs. They have yet to tap into their power and competence. Whether holding the reins tightly or loosely, it's about finding the balance and applying the right amount of pressure.

If you constantly feel the need to get permission to act, you might need to examine your relationship with authority. If you are concerned that your boss, spouse, or peers won't approve of your actions, you tend to freeze and do nothing. This is an example of being in a one-down relationship with authority. Mature adults make decisions without needing to ask for permission.

Another reason to explore your relationship to authority is if you respond to those in authority over you (compliant) entirely differently from those under your authority (tyrannical). Developed leaders balance the ability to easily submit to their upward chain of command while offering supportive leadership to those who report to them. Submission can be a loaded word and works best in "power with" and "power to" dynamics. Outside of that, the relationship is imbalanced, and power struggle issues occur. Adults have a healthy respect for leaders and find it easy to follow directions or orders. Good leaders make great followers.

Connections and experiences from early childhood to the present day inform your leadership skills. Identifying patterns in relationships is very helpful for your personal development. Notice the places where you feel the need to make yourself BIG when expressing your point of view. Do you ever find your emotions escalating when trying to get your point across? You might blurt out your thoughts with too much enthusiasm or choose to say nothing. You notice your heart rate escalating, your palms sweating, and your words get stuck in your throat. You ask yourself if you should speak up or remain silent.

Finding your voice is an essential leadership trait. Having the confidence to express your thoughts even when contrary to popular opinion is a sign of an independent and self-assured individual. Creating the space for others to do the same is the sign of a great leader.

Holding the reins effectively requires asserting the proper amount of authority. It's about being in the right relationship with yourself and others, which means being comfortable submitting to the leaders you report to and supporting those who report to you.

Three strategies to help ensure that you aren't holding the reins too tightly or loosely include:

- Develop self-awareness
- Take responsibility for yourself, and
- Allow mutual exchanges in your relationships

When facing difficult situations, notice physical symptoms like sweaty palms or a racing heart. Do you find it challenging to speak up, or maybe you plead your case like a desperate teenager desiring an extended curfew?

This is a great time to get feedback on how others perceive you. Check-in with someone from your life team or a coach. Many find their inner thoughts and dialog harsher than how others experience them. Sometimes, our thoughts about ourselves need to be silenced, and other times, they need to be validated. Optimal self-awareness comes from a mature personal perspective alongside input from trusted, reliable sources.

Another strategy is to own your actions and outcomes. Leaders understand the impact that their decisions have on others. They take ownership of their views on religion, politics, finances, and leadership. Blaming circumstances or others should always be avoided.

Invite others to be heard. Practice speaking up to those in authority over you. Be aware of parent-child dynamics, where you find yourself talking down to someone or you show up feeling inferior. Seek quality in relationships, not control. The most evolved and effective leaders stand in their authority without holding the reins too tightly or loosely and empower others to do the same.

What's Your Next Pinnacle Moment?

The journey to a pinnacle moment isn't always easy, but the destination is a powerful motivator. It's a chance to push your limits, discover your strengths, and create a memory that will forever shape who you are.

So, what audacious goal will you set for yourself next?

Don't be afraid to dream big. Identify your intrinsic motivators, build a supportive team, and embrace the challenges along the way. Remember, every pinnacle moment starts with a single step. I look forward to seeing what BHAG Max and Angel accomplish next.

See you at the finish line! -KM

***

To contact Kristi:

visit kristimallory.com

LinkedIn @KristiMallory

FB and IG @KristiMalloryCoaching

Vivian Shapiro

Vivian Shapiro is an energetic, positive-minded influencer, grateful to be active and vibrant, while heading into her 80s! Recently she became an Amazon International Best-Selling Author for both her contributions to the multi authored books ***Entangled No More*** and ***Soulful Poems***. In June 2023, she achieved Bestseller status again for her first solo book, ***Go Vibrant! ...notes & anecdotes on loving and living the joie de VIVre.*** In ***The Change***, she contributes her passion to empower readers to find the joy and vibrancy within their lives.

Vivian is a writer of music, children's books, plays, poetry, as well as a singer, actor, dancer, choreographer and more!

A Toronto teacher, VP and Principal, and later Education Director of a charity for youth, she developed and spearheaded leadership programs and conferences for disenfranchised young people. She is a recipient of the 2012 *"Amazing Aces in Action Award",* and the 2018 *"Celebrating Outstanding Women Award for Philanthropy"* both for her work with the Herbert H. Carnegie Future Aces Foundation and in the community.

As an Independent Consultant with Arbonne International, she coaches and trains people to create a life of choice and abundance, helping them defy aging by immersing themselves in a healthy lifestyle, no matter their gender or age. As a mom to a blended family, she loves engaging as "vava" to her thirteen grandchildren! She sees herself as the shining light to help be the spark for others.

Grow Your Vibe! Glow Vitality! Go Vibrant!

By Vivian Shapiro

When things are meant to be…

There it was yet again. That phrase: *"I want to be you when I grow up*!" followed by the question, *"Viv, how do you do it? Where do you get that energy and how do you stay so vibrant?*" I was reconnecting with a friend I had not seen for over fifteen years. After engaging in a very lively discussion, Robyn looked into my eyes and added, *"No really, Viv! I want to know. What is your secret sauce?*" Of course, I was flattered.

It's been something I have heard many times, since I was in my forties and fortunately even at 79 at the time of this writing, I still do. This time was different. I decided to find my magic formula so that I could share it!

That evening, I went into a deep and serious self-study to find out the answers to my questions:

- "Why do people say that to me?"
- "Who was I?"
- "What was I still meant to do?
- "What is it that I did or continue to do to live vibrantly?
- "How have I lived my life to present myself as a person others want to emulate?"

Previously I had succumbed to my own view of myself as insecure, needy, self-deprecating, compulsive, type A, a perfectionist, sometimes controlling, and even a bit bitchy. I know that I can be too much for people, much too much. Fortunately, many friends, family and acquaintances tried to open my eyes to my gifts that fill my heart with pride and make me realize I have "some 'splaining to do", as Ricky would often say to Lucy! I was now ready to honour me and explain proudly.

I was up for the task; I was ready to plunge into the core of me to discover what I was truly all about. What were the characteristics, the attributes that made me stand out as *Vibrant* to others? What was my secret sauce? Correction: What IS my secret sauce?

These questions propelled me to enter the doorway to my stash of over forty plus journals. Started over 40 years ago, their covers have more colours than Joseph's coat!

My journals have been my best friends. They allow me to say or tell stories about anything! They don't judge, they do not deliver marks for literary prowess, and best of all they don't answer back! Within their covers, I made promises to myself, where I allowed my deepest thoughts and feelings to erupt with no real intention other than perhaps to release them. Journalling was and is a way for me to bring my adventures to life, make honest comments about events, and to bring my artistic skills to the fore, especially that of my poetic self. Truthfully and sadly, I had not spent much time checking in with my past self that was speaking to my future self. I decided it was now time to dedicate myself to pouring myself into my words and reliving my truths.

I couldn't wait to venture down the multicoloured road of "Journal Land" to find my VIBRANT SELF and discover the MAGIC of ME! (And whatever other things I would uncover.) Gleefully, I went on this journey with my highlighters, sticky notes and my backpack full of additional questions to conquer the quest for my magic sauce.

Perhaps I could find something worth sharing with the world. Perhaps there was a gift in the many words and thoughts poured into these pages that might help someone find their truer self. I was about to find out. First the purpose was to find my own true self!

When looking at yourself through objective eyes…

Before me lay a combination of tender, heartbreaking, happy, angry, sensitive stories of every kind of genre and subject; my own personal thoughts on living, learning, loving, in a variety of forms; beautiful, sad, angry, funny excerpts; clever poems, both rhyming and free verse; ideas for songs; rough drafts of songs; "Vivianisms"; sketches; drawings; favourite lines; personal paintings, and portraits.

I was stunned when I read through them, surprisingly impressed at my writing ability and sensitivity. As I dove deep into my journals, keeping my modesty in my back pocket, I congratulated myself on how perceptive and enlightening I sounded!

I found several qualities that repeatedly stood out among both the happy times and the angry bitter experiences. I found I could fill up the letters of VIBRANT to create an acronym, and oh how I love acronyms! I was VIBRANT with experiences full of love, losses and lessons! That's when the book that I was meant to write appeared to me in a vision! The timing was perfect.

When a vision becomes clear…

My mission was clear. I would reveal my secret sauce while leaving a legacy for my family. I imagined my purpose and my intention. I now had answers and stories I was ready to share. I was uncovering the secret sauce within myself that gave credence and life to my vibrant being. I possessed a formula I was ready to gift!

And thus, my book ***Go Vibrant! … notes and anecdotes on living and loving the joie de VIVr*e,**

and its new budding author, was born, labour pains and all!

I had many moments of imposter syndrome, wondering *"Who am I to write a book to tell others how to live*?" while the superhero in me counteracted with *"Who are you not to?"* RIGHT? Damn Right!

I wish to share with you here the V.I.B.R.A.N.T. magic sauce which isn't so magic after all!

I do not profess to be an advisor, a coach, a psychiatrist, a preacher, a social worker, a healer, a therapist or a celebrity writing their memoirs. What I am is a lover of life, an observer of opportunities, a scriber of stories, an editor of experiences, a singer of songs, a ponderer of poetry, an empath of everything, a feeler of fantasies, a masseuse of messages, a teacher of thoughts, a dealer of dreams.

I am, in fact, just like you. I am just an ordinary person with ordinary experiences, yet extraordinary messages that may help one find strategies for a happier, more joyful, engaging and truer you, living a life you control, a life in which you will be empowered to rise above, no matter the entanglements.

Why would you want to live vibrantly? I invite you to read the full book available on Amazon, (check my contact info) and find out! In the meantime, let's look at this secret sauce as I break down each letter of V.I.B.R.A.N.T., into the attributes that kept me empowered, adding a few meaningful anecdotes as I watch carefully my word count!

V: Viva La Vs

- Be a VISIONARY
- Find your unique VIBE
- Practice VISUALIZATION
- Create your VIBRATION
- Know and live your VALUES
- Add VALUE to others

Being a Visionary

Even at the age of 5, I seemed to have had an extraordinarily huge VISION of what life was meant to be for me. But I did not know that at the time.

Did you play school when you were young? I loved to be the "teacher" and would convince my other friends that they should be the students. Somehow, they agreed! When more joined, I assigned myself to the role of "principal" when I didn't even really know what the role even meant. All I knew was that it was bigger, better and more important than being a student or teacher! As a young child I VISUALIZED myself at the top!

The fact that I lived with a huge VISION as a child, was a bit of a dichotomy between the "reality" me and the "virtual" me. As an immigrant from Europe with Jewish parents from Germany who escaped the holocaust, living together with my "Omi" and "Opi", born in Portugal, but with German speaking parents and grandparents, I was a bit of an oddity. The first preschool I attended back in the late 1940s in Toronto was not as it is today, alive with mixed ethnicities, cultures and colours. I was cute but I was odd.

My parents worked long hours while I lived with my very critical and scary grandmother who was severely scarred by the unfortunate personal trials she lived and witnessed in Nazi Germany. She had watched firsthand the loss of family and was pressured to quickly escape her beloved home. Not knowing any of this, as a young child, I feared her.

I grew up introverted, afraid to speak my broken English and extremely insecure among others. However, on my own, the "virtual" me dreamed big! Big bold gargantuan dreams!

We moved often to different Canadian cities following my dad's career journey. This constant change of friends, schools and communities did not help my self-image. Thanks to books and places my parents took me, I visualized myself being a great dancer, artist, actor, singer, creatively thinking of me in all sorts of imaginative ways. All this before the impact of television or social media!

We moved a total of six times until my parents settled for a permanent home. I was thrilled! I had attended six different schools from ages 4 to 12. Not a great way to accumulate long-term lifelong friends! I remember, however, despite being bullied, teased, chosen last for teams and not always being invited to the "popular" parties, I loved life. I may have been sad or confused, crying myself to sleep some nights, but I also remember smiling, dancing and laughing a lot!

I had other challenges. I was tagged with cruel names like "Four Eyes" as I sported corrective glasses at the end of Grade 3. "Bucky Beaver" was my other "nom de plume" because of my very large front teeth and conspicuous overbite. Most kids or teachers could not pronounce my strange German last name (Leinung). I absolutely hated my first name Vivian. I wanted so badly to be Mary Catherine or Jane or Sally like most of the other girls!

Despite all of this, I loved to laugh, sing, dance, act and play and I absolutely loved school. I guess I was smart. I had that going for me! I "skipped" Grade 4 and was accelerated from Grade 3 to Grade 5. This may not have been wise, given as a late November birth baby, I was already younger than most of the students. I don't know what they were thinking in those days! Later in university that age difference caught up to me!

The main fact was that being able to **visualize** on my own created for me a place where I was revered, admired, beautiful, respected and loved. Those visualizations were my wings to lift me to a place of validation.

Today as a much more spiritual being, I look back and thank those days of challenge I had as a young toddler and pre-teen. They say your setbacks set you up for your setups. They were, in fact, a blessing, as the many incidents led me to a world of dreams and desires that superseded any of the hurt or initial tears.

My dad of course was heartbroken to see his first child upset. But my mom? A force of nature! She was the domineering alpha in our family. What she did for me was equally as loving as my dad but in a much different way. She did affirm that I was beautiful and smart and that I could be anything I wanted to be. She encouraged me to move on, to not dwell on negative experiences and to think other thoughts with promises that my tomorrows would bring a new day. In other words: Get over it! Shit happens. Some downs, some ups, so what…next!

I grew strong in my conviction to be someone special and later, as a teacher and principal, had huge empathy for any student going through similar situations.

What steered me to live vibrantly? No matter what age, what circumstance, having a VISION of what things can be, can alter your life. Happy visions, healthy mind.

I recommend you practice *visualizing*! We are all born with a vivid sense of imagination! Just watch a child playing with cardboard boxes or plastic containers. Along with self-satisfying visualizations, using your imagination along with your wisdom allows you to think beyond your own dreams, to the deeper level of envisioning a better world to make a difference for others. Find your true purpose as a *visionary* to enhance your life as you serve others. This will without a doubt keep you *vibrant* with purpose to find your *vibe* and honour your *values.*

I: Inviting the Is

- Invite your I AM
- IMAGINE
- Have INTERESTS
- Be INTERESTED and INTERESTING
- Set INTENTIONS
- Be INSPIRED and INSPIRING
- Live with INTEGRITY

Invite your "I AM"!

Being vibrant can only occur when you look after the "I" in your life… as in me myself and I! Let's discover the most important aspect of vibrancy…YOU! The "I" you bring to this world, the intimate "I", the unique, wonderful "I" that defines the special awesome you!

Some may call me over-extended, but I honestly believe that keeping busy keeps you living with vitality so that you can put your best foot forward as a vibrant, exciting, *interesting* person who can't wait to start each day, looking forward to *inspiring* others and having an impact and influence on the world.

"'I AM' are the 2 most powerful words you can use to start a sentence"

- Dr. Wayne W. Dyer

B: So B it!

- Be BOLD
- Be (you)
- Be BRAVE
- BELIEVE
- Be BODACIOUS
- Be a BADASS

Just for fun, fill this out. Don't overthink it. Just fill out the acronym for BOLD with whatever comes to mind!

To Live My VIBRANT life means BEING BOLD by:

B ______________________________

O ______________________________

L ______________________________

D ______________________________

Here's mine: To Live My VIBRANT life means BEING BOLD by:

B **Believing** enough in my talents, skills and abilities that I know I can try anything!

O **Opening** up my mind to all that's possible!

L **Listening** to what leaders do to be successful

D **Discarding** and **Dismissing Debbie Doubt** whenever she interferes!

Imagine your comfort zone

It is a full length zippered hooded coat from head to ankles. Unzip it slowly one zip at a time. Visualize this. See various parts of your mind and body emerging into a world where you are free to *be* you, free to be *bold*, *brave*, *bodacious*, and even a *badass*, free to try out new things, boldly stepping forth to new worlds of *being*. What an exhilarating feeling it is to discover what's outside your comfort zone!

R: Roar those Rs

- ROAR your being
- RECHARGE your energy
- Engage in ROUTINES and RITUALS
- Show RESILIENCE
- Radiate RADIANCE
- REFLECT on Self

- Use ROSE-COLOURED GLASSES

Rrrrroar!

To start and continue to ROAR with the energy you need to live life, you must take responsibility for your own resurrection, *recharging* and rejuvenation, should you encounter challenges, setbacks or unwelcome experiences. For me as I matured, I realized that having a spiritual and self-care *routine* and *ritual*, specifically in the morning, assisted me to be able to pause, breathe and *reflect*, handle the unexpected and *radiate* my radiance! What's yours?

A: Ace the As

- Take ACTION
- Be ADVENTUROUS
- Seek ACHIEVEMENTS
- Live AUDACIOUSLY
- Create ABUNDANCE
- Have an ATTITUDE of GRATITUDE

Lights, Camera Action!

To lead a *VIBRANT* life, I encourage you to be *ACTION* oriented. *Action* leads to *Adventures*.

Adventures lead to *Achievements*. Achievements no matter how big or small attract others and events into your life.

In the words of motivational speaker Jim Rohn:

"You are the average of the five people you spend the most time with."

Attracting others brings you *Abundance*.

Abundance leads you to an appreciation, an acceptance and love of yourself and others.

And an *Attitude* of gratitude completes the portrait.

N: Start with the N Game in Mind

- NURTURE Yourself
- NOURISH Yourself
- Learn to say NO
- Be one with NATURE
- Find your NIRVANA
- Be NAUGHTY
- Be NICE
- Be a tad NUTS

Being Naked with Nature

I learned at a very early age that being one with nature was healing. Country life surrounded by nature, family and friends was refreshing, revitalizing and such fun! I learned a lot about life during the summer months spent at relative's cottages. The lake replaced the ocean in Portugal for me. I learned to fish, row a boat, run a small motorboat, canoe, swim and dive off rocks at a very early age. I learned to water ski, first standing on a handmade wide wooden board (the original wakeboard) until I graduated to two skis and then eventually slalom. But most of all I learned to dream, reflect, plan, write, paint, find my *nirvana*, *nurture* my thoughts, sometimes *naughty*, *nice* and *nuts*! I still love what I call "being naked in nature!" I take in the thrill of it all, except the mosquitos!

COTTAGE PESTS by Vivian Shapiro 2004

I'd give away my chocolate

I'd never eat fajitas

If someone would remove from here

The spiders and mosquitoes

T: Fits You to a T

- Be a TENACIOUS TRAILBLAZER

- Get your vibe from your TRIBE
- Try TENDERNESS
- Select your TEAM to compliment you
- Choose TOGETHERNESS
- Be TRUE to forgiveness
- Be THANKFUL

Tough, yet tender with tenacity

Tenacity in life can help you keep up a vibrant, sprightly, high-spirited life.

If someone calls you tenacious, you're probably the kind of person who never gives up and never stops trying; someone who does whatever is required to accomplish a goal or to get through hurdles or challenges, never allowing yourself to be discouraged, moving on and forward. By family members you may be seen as being stubborn, but you are a go-getter, unstoppably vibrant!

Only in reading my journals about my thoughts of determination, moving forward when challenges came my way, do I now realize that I, in fact, lived with a tenacity of which I was not even aware. Always *thankful* for my blessings in life, that and my supportive *team* of family and friends kept me going!

As best you can, through good times, low moments and deepest of funks, focus on remaining…

V *a Visionary with Vitality*

I *an Inspirer and Influencer*

B *a Bold Boss babe*

R *a Resilient and Radiant force*

A *an Action-oriented Achiever*

N *a Nurturing soul, searching your Nirvana*

T *a Tenacious Trailblazer Thankful for your Tribe*

I notice in my life two types of people in the world: those who choose to be vibrant and live with positivity, joy and vitality, and those who choose to be apathetic, dull, and negative. Of course there are varying degrees of each category. For me, you either lean one way or the other.

Truth bomb: joy and happiness doesn't come from fame, fortune, or material possessions! Happiness comes from within. Happy people choose to make themselves happy by creating joy in their life and living vibrantly!

As an intentional impactor and agent for change, I love to help others. I act with courage to release fear, anger, and apathy knowing these do not serve me. I activate my light not only for myself but for others. I know that if I fulfill my potential, I can show others how to do so. I want you to believe in YOU and that you can purposefully bring on that VIBRANT life no matter your age or circumstances! I invite you to unwrap the gift of vibrance I have carefully tied with a glorious ribbon. Find the hidden attributes you possess!

We are stars wrapped in skin.

The light you are seeking has always been within

- Rumi

Hello Readers. I would love to hear from you if you are interested in conversing with me or asking me questions about my books or my side business. I make a lively podcast guest or speaker! If you would just like to get to know me better, chat and exchange stories, you can contact me in any way you choose!

***

Cheers, Vivian Shapiro

cell: 416-726-9210 (Toronto Canada)

email: vivianshapiro@rogers.com

personal website: http://www.vivianshapiro.com

insta: vibrantvivianshapiro

fb: Vivian Shapiro

Arbonne IC website http://www.vivandamanda.arbonne.com

Arbonne biz video: https://youtu.be/SkTviz3pg5I?si=jzJnMeDH-m3CxFU9

Amazon Best Selling Author:

Go Vibrant! .. notes & anecdotes on loving and living the joie de VIVre

Canada

https://a.co/d/7WNRec0

United States

https://kdp.amazon.com/amazon-dp-action/us/dualbookshelf.marketplacelink/B0C6W2YW7

Tina K Kailea

Tina K Kailea is a feminine business mentor, embodiment coach, bestselling author, book doula, and international speaker — a wild executive at heart.

As the founder of Femmepreneur Pathfinder, Tina is on a mission to inspire women to take bold action. She empowers them to claim what they desire, say NO without hesitation, set boundaries without guilt, and fully embody the essence of who they are as an extension of their brand.

Known for her unapologetic and rebellious spirit, Tina is passionate about supporting female leaders in breaking free from limiting beliefs and shattering their 'not-good-enough' mindset. She guides women to embrace their full potential by overcoming the subconscious conditioning that holds them back, allowing them to lead with confidence and authenticity.

Tina's unique approach blends business acumen and intuitive mentorship with deep personal transformation, encouraging her clients to step into their true power. She creates a safe and nourishing environment where women can redefine what it means to be both feminine and powerful, balancing strength and vulnerability.

Her work is about more than just achieving success; it's about helping women live and lead with integrity, fully aligned with their values and soul's purpose.

Tina is the author of the bestselling and award-winning book CORPORATE REWILDING – A Wild Woman's Guide to Reclaiming Your Feminine Power, available worldwide on Amazon.

The Feminine Reset: Escape Corporate Burnout and Reclaim Your Life

by Tina K Kailea

This chapter is for you—the woman who feels like something is missing, who longs to break free from the endless cycle of "doing" and rediscover what it means to simply *be*, but who feels unsure about how to take the next step. You've achieved so much, yet you find yourself longing for something deeper, something more fulfilling. I'm here to tell you that you're not alone.

I've been where you are, and I've found a way through.

Have you been functioning on autopilot just to get through, trying to be everything for everyone else, and somewhere along the way, you lost yourself? I remember what it feels like to be so disconnected from your own body, your desires, and your purpose that you wonder if you'll ever feel truly alive again.

You're exhausted, unfulfilled, and have a deep longing for the woman you used to be. The pressure to do it all is slowly suffocating your spirit, leaving little room for joy, intimacy, or connection. You're running on fumes.

If you're reading this, chances are you can relate. You've achieved great things, but it's come at a cost. You feel exhausted, burnt out, and miles away from the vibrant woman you once were.

I've walked in your shoes. I know what it feels like to be "successful" yet utterly unhappy with yourself and your life. I was once the woman who seemed to have it all—a successful career, a six-figure salary, and a life that looked perfect on paper. But underneath it all, I was crumbling, suffocated by the very life I had worked so hard to build. I've experienced that sense of disillusionment—the exhaustion that seeps into your bones and drains your energy, the dissatisfaction that creeps into your heart when you realize the life you've built is not the one you truly want.

I want to share my story with you, not because I have all the answers, but because I've been where you are. I've walked through the fire, and gotten to the other side, I found a life that is rich, joyful, fulfilling, and deeply aligned with who I am at my core. I no longer wear a mask.

I want you to give yourself permission to admit that you may be trapped in a life that doesn't feel like your own. In this chapter, I'll take you through the steps that helped me reclaim my feminine power and create a life I love. My hope is that my story will inspire you to take the first steps toward your own transformation.

1. The Corporate Burnout Trap: How Success is Silently Draining You

Success—it's what we've been taught to chase from the moment we enter the workforce. Promotions, raises, recognition—it all looks like the dream. But for women like us, it often comes at a steep price. We push ourselves harder and harder, striving for perfection, trying to prove that we belong in spaces dominated by masculine energy.

But something shifts when we stay there for too long. You feel it in your body—the fatigue, the sleepless nights. You've forgotten what it feels like to be you. You feel alienated from your relationships, like the spark that once existed with your partner has faded. You tell yourself you'll make time for intimacy, for fun, for relaxation—when things slow down.

Except they never do.

I know how it feels to wake up and wonder how you ended up here living a life that feels more like survival than living. You've been pushing, striving, giving all of yourself to your career, and now…there's barely anything left for you.

I was there too. In my early years as a General Manager at an international publishing company, I worked tirelessly to prove my worth. I told myself that the accolades, the money, and the power would make me happy. And for a while, they did. But as time went on, I noticed something: the harder I worked, the more disconnected I became—from my body, my emotions, and the people I loved.

I had become a machine, ignoring the signs my body was giving me. Anxiety, depression, and adrenal fatigue crept in. Then, a series of personal tragedies—five miscarriages—shattered me both physically and emotionally. I had spent years pursuing a version of success that wasn't mine. It was eroding me and, as a result, my body deemed it unsafe to carry a pregnancy to full term.

The success I had worked so hard for left me burnt out, isolated, and empty. I had hit rock bottom, and my body was silently screaming at me. I knew something had to change. That's when I made a shift—not just in my career, but in the way I lived, how I saw myself, and how I embraced my power as a woman.

2. Reawakening Yourself: Reconnecting with Your Feminine Energy

There was a time when I looked in the mirror and didn't even recognize the woman staring back at me. I had given everything to my career, to being the "strong one", to being the woman who could do it all. But I had lost myself in the process.

The term "reawakening" entered my life during this dark period, and it saved me. It refers to reconnecting with your wild, natural, authentic self—the feminine essence that we, as women, often suppress to fit into a world designed for masculine structure. We're taught to lead with logic, power through exhaustion, and ignore the whispers of our intuition.

But the truth is, there is incredible power in the feminine. It's intuitive, creative, nurturing, and deeply connected to the flow of life. Reawakening is about reclaiming that power and living in alignment with it.

For me, this meant stepping back from the corporate grind and spending time reevaluating everything—reconnecting with my body. I started small. I carved out time in the morning to breathe, to journal, to move my body in ways that felt nourishing. I let go of the need to constantly be productive and began to trust that rest was just as important as action. The more I leaned into my feminine energy, the more alive I felt. With that aliveness came clarity. I realized I didn't have to sacrifice my health, relationships, or joy to be successful. I could have both.

Reawakening isn't about abandoning goals or ambition; it's about realigning your life so your drive for success doesn't drain you but energizes you. It's about tapping into the softness, wisdom, and sensuality of your feminine nature, allowing it to guide you in your career and relationships without compromise.

You deserve more than just survival. You deserve to live, to thrive, to feel deeply alive in every part of your being. The only thing standing between you and that life is the choice to say yes to yourself.

3. Practical Strategies for Reawakening Your Life

Reawakening is about integrating your feminine energy into your life in a way that brings balance and fulfilment. Here are some steps that helped me reconnect with my feminine power:

Reconnect with Your Body

After years of pushing through exhaustion, your body needs your attention. Start small—whether it's a daily yoga practice, a walk in nature, or simply taking a few minutes to breathe and check in with yourself. Notice where you're holding tension and allow yourself to release it.

Our bodies are where we experience life, but in the hustle of daily demands, we often disconnect from them. When was the last time you listened to your body's needs? It's time to reconnect, to feel your body and acknowledge it as your ally in this journey.

Create Space for Stillness

In a world that celebrates constant action, stillness is radical. Take 5-10 minutes each day to be still. This can be through meditation, journaling, or simply sitting in silence. It's in these moments that your true desires will start to emerge.

You might resist this at first—your mind will race, telling you that you don't have time to sit and do nothing. But in that stillness is where your answers live. Your intuition, your clarity, your wild feminine power all come through when you make space to hear them.

When you stop the constant doing, you'll hear the soft, quiet voice inside you—your inner knowing—beginning to speak again. What does she say? What is it that you truly need, crave, and desire? The more stillness you create, the louder that voice will become, guiding you toward the life you're meant to live.

Redefine Success

Success isn't just about career achievements. It's about feeling fulfilled, balanced, and joyful. Take some time to reflect on what success really means to you—not what society tells you it should be. What would your life look like if you were thriving, not just surviving?

The success we've been taught to chase is often rooted in external validation—climbing the corporate ladder, gaining recognition, earning more money. But what if success wasn't about what you achieved but how you feel in your body, your relationships, and your spirit?

Ask yourself: What do I truly want? Let go of the narrow definition of success you've been holding onto and create a vision of success that is uniquely yours.

Set Boundaries

One of the hardest but most important lessons I learned was the power of saying no. As women, we're conditioned to be people-pleasers, but this often leads to burnout. Start practicing saying no to things that drain your energy and yes to things that nourish you.

Setting boundaries isn't about being selfish; it's about protecting your energy so you can show up fully for the things that matter most. Boundaries are an act of self-love and protect your well-being. Every time you say yes to something that doesn't align with your values; you're saying no to yourself. Start small and practice saying no to that extra project at work or social events that don't serve you. With each boundary you set, you'll begin to feel lighter, freer, and more in control of your life.

Surround Yourself with Support

Reawakening isn't something you have to do alone. Find a community of like-minded women who can support you on your journey. Whether it's through women's circles, masterminds, or retreats, having a support system is essential.

When you surround yourself with women who are also on this journey of reclaiming their power, you'll feel less alone, more supported, and infinitely more capable of creating the life you truly desire. There's something incredibly powerful about being in the presence of women who are committed to living authentically, who understand your struggles, and who will cheer you on as you step into your feminine power.

4. Embracing Feminine Leadership: Impact Without Losing Yourself

For so long, I believed leadership meant pushing through, powering on, and always staying one step ahead. But as I began to reconnect with my feminine energy, I realized true leadership isn't about hustle—it's about alignment. It's about leading from a place of vulnerability, intuition, and connection, rather than constant striving.

Feminine leadership is powerful because it allows you to lead with empathy, collaboration, and authenticity. It's about trusting your intuition, listening to your team, and creating an environment where people feel seen, heard, and valued.

I realized that by stepping into my feminine power, I could create far more impact than I ever could through sheer force. I no longer needed to prove myself through constant hustle. Instead, I led with ease and grace, trusting that I'm enough just the way I am.

When we lead from our feminine essence, we lead from the heart. This doesn't diminish our strength—it amplifies it. We become leaders who are not only successful but also fulfilled, aligned, and deeply connected to their purpose. This is the kind of leadership that inspires others, not through fear or dominance but through authenticity and compassion.

5. Reclaiming Your Relationships: Finding Intimacy & Connection Again

One of the most painful consequences of my corporate burnout was the impact it had on my relationships. I was so consumed by work that I barely had time or energy to connect with the people I loved, including my husband. Intimacy had become a distant memory, and the disconnection between us grew wider with each passing day.

When you're caught in the cycle of burnout, relationships can often feel like another item on the to-do list. You're too exhausted to engage deeply, too overwhelmed to be present, and too removed from yourself to connect meaningfully with others. You might even feel guilty because you know you're not showing up the way you want to, but you just don't have the capacity.

Reawakening isn't just about reconnecting with yourself—it's about reconnecting with others. As I began to honor my own needs and embrace my feminine energy, I noticed a shift in my mood and my relationships. I made time for intimacy, not just physical but emotional as well. I learned to be present with my husband, to truly listen and connect, rather than being distracted by the never-ending demands of work.

Here's the truth: intimacy and connection aren't luxuries—they're vital to living a fulfilled life. By reconnecting with yourself, you can begin to rebuild the emotional and physical connection with your partner. It doesn't happen overnight, but small acts of presence and vulnerability can reignite the spark.

6. The Power of Sisterhood: Finding Support in Like-Minded Women

For too long, I believed that I had to go it alone. I was fiercely independent, believing that asking for help was a sign of weakness. But as I began to change, I realized there is incredible power in sisterhood.

I started attending women's circles—places where I could show up vulnerably and be seen for who I truly was. These circles became my sanctuary—a place where I could release the weight of perfectionism and simply *be*. The support of women who were on similar journeys gave me the courage to keep going, even when the path was hard.

Sisterhood isn't about competition; it's about collaboration, connection, and deep, unconditional support. When you surround yourself with other women who dare to show up vulnerably, something magical happens. You realize you're not alone. You see your struggles mirrored in others, and in that reflection, you find strength.

When you step into a circle of women who are committed to living in their power, you are reminded of your own. In sisterhood, we rise together.

7. The Road to Reawakening: Where Will You Begin?

As I look back on my journey, I'm filled with gratitude for the woman I've become. It wasn't easy, and there were times when I wanted to give up. But by trusting myself, embodying more of my feminine energy, and surrounding myself with support, I was able to create a life that feels true to who I am.

Now, it's your turn!

You don't have to make a massive change overnight. Start small. Take one step toward reawakening your life—whether it's through reconnecting with your body, setting boundaries, or finding a community of women who understand you.

Ask yourself: What would my life look like if I chose to honor my needs? What could change if I allowed myself to be supported by others? How would it feel to lead from a place of feminine strength rather than burnout?

Remember, you are not alone in this journey. The path to reclaiming your wild feminine power is a deeply personal one, but it's also a path that many women have walked before you. We are here, cheering you on, reminding you that you are powerful beyond measure.

So, where will you begin?

Key Takeaways

Reawakening is about reconnecting with your natural feminine energy, not abandoning your ambitions.

Success is about alignment, balance, and joy—not just career achievements.

Practical steps like reconnecting with your body, creating stillness, and setting boundaries can help you reclaim your power.

Feminine leadership allows you to create more impact without losing yourself in the process.

Reconnecting with yourself will lead to deeper, more fulfilling relationships.

Sisterhood is essential—find a community that supports your journey.

The road to reawakening starts with small, actionable steps. Take the first step today.

Final Thought

This journey of reclaiming your feminine power isn't about perfection—it's about progress. It's about giving yourself permission to live in alignment with who you truly are, without the fear of falling short or the pressure of maintaining a façade.

I know how hard it can be to take that first step, to trust that things can be different. But trust me when I say that the life you crave—the one where you feel alive, vibrant, and powerful—is possible. It's waiting for you.

So, are you ready? Are you ready to stop settling for a life that feels empty? Are you ready to reclaim the parts of yourself you've lost along the way—the parts that make you feel whole, alive, and fully you?

This is your moment. Right now, you have the power to choose differently. To say yes to yourself, to step into your feminine strength, and to create a life that nourishes your soul. I'm inviting you to take that first step. You don't have to do it alone—I'm here to guide you every step of the way.

The choice is yours—and it's time to choose you.

Please reach out to connect. I'd love to help you on your journey to Feminine R.E.S.E.T. and I'd be honored to walk this path with you.

Tina K Kailea

***

To contact Tina:

International Speaker, Award-wining Author, Feminine Mindset Strategist, & Possibility Agent

Website: www.femmepreneurpathfinder.com

LinkedIn: https://www.linkedin.com/in/tinakkailea

Facebook: https://www.facebook.com/tinakkailea

Instagram: https://www.instagram.com/the_femmepreneur

Link for LinkTree:
https://www.femmepreneurpathfinder.com/instagram

Gift - Free Mindset Magic eGuide:
https://www.femmepreneurpathfinder.com/free-eguide-download

Jessica Rice

Jessica Rice is The Vision Evolution Coach™, a certified ICF coach, speaker, entrepreneur, and host of the Hello You Show podcast. She is focused on helping visionary leaders create a lasting legacy they love.

With over 15 years in tech and high-profile government with an emphasis on design, engineering, and corporate leadership, Jessica found her calling the first time she experienced coaching. She has been on a mission ever since to help others achieve the same transformative results through the profound impact professional coaching delivers.

Jessica is an executive leadership and business coach dedicated to helping her clients rise up and reach their next-level goals and unique vision for their lives. She has studied under some of the best coaches and leaders in the industry with a focus on transformational leadership, executive presence, neuroscience, and business strategy.

She has worked with a range of clients in a variety of industries, including top leaders in tech, government, and biosciences, as well as business leaders in creative arts, health and fitness, and holistic wellness. Her greatest joy comes from watching her clients discover their golden path toward creating a life of meaning and purpose that they truly love.

Jessica is a native to California and is a wife, mom, stepmom, and pet parent. She homeschools their son and enjoys visiting the ocean and forests near her home.

Bold Moves: Becoming a Silent Disruptor of Change in Your Life

By Jessica Rice

One morning, after another sleepless night, I woke up exhausted—physically and emotionally. Lost in a career that no longer felt right, I looked in the mirror and realized I had a choice: continue on this unfulfilling path or reclaim control of my life.

Have you ever woken up with a feeling of despair, with the same routine ahead of you, the struggles in your job, conversations with your boss, and the next fire to put out? Sometimes, it can feel like we cannot create the life we want because we are in too deep and the effort to change feels insurmountable.

I'm here to tell you it doesn't have to be this way. You can still lead a life that excites and drives you to create a legacy you adore. Change is not only possible; it's within your reach.

"The purpose of life is not to be happy. It is to be useful, to be honorable, to be compassionate, to have it make some difference that you have lived and lived well." – Ralph Waldo Emerson

Our daily choice.

Every morning brings a new opportunity—an open door to change, growth, and possibilities. But the key lies in recognizing that the power to unlock it has always been within you.

Change is inevitable, but it's never too late to embrace it. Even when it feels hard, you can continually rethink how you show up each day and what habits you create to live a life of bold purpose. While rewiring your mind is challenging, it's entirely possible to rethink how you show up each day, what you believe is possible, and what new habits you can create to live a life of bold purpose.

The question for most of us is really: How?

How do you actually create change for yourself when it feels like you are too deep in your career, your life is full of unending expectations, you have made more than your fair share of mistakes, and you didn't seize opportunities that would have carved a different path when you had the chance.

We often confuse hope with regret, not realizing that regret teaches us lessons from our past, while hope is the beacon that guides us toward change.

So do the thing that scares you the most. Isn't that what regret ought to teach us?

Why, then, do we still stay stuck?

Fear—of failure, disappointment, or change—keeps us stuck. We cling to the familiar because it feels safe, even when it's unfulfilling. But in doing so, we lose trust in ourselves.

Why trust is the secret to success.

But fear, while potent, is not insurmountable. The key to moving past it is to build something even more substantial: trust. Trust in yourself is the bedrock upon which all growth is constructed. It's what makes you feel secure and confident in your journey.

A few elements establish personal trust over time: *reliability, communication, empathy, authenticity, integrity, gratitude, nonjudgment, positive relationships, accountability, competency, and transparency.*

If you were to look at each of these elements and ask yourself, "How am I doing in building trust with myself," what would be revealed?

Take inventory of how you create trust with yourself and ask the following questions:

1. How do I demonstrate that I am reliable and dependable to myself and others?
2. How do I communicate to myself and others in words and actions?
3. How do I continue to show up authentically in my life?
4. How do I show empathy for myself and others?

5. How do I demonstrate my integrity with the way I show up in the world?

6. How do I show appreciation for others and myself?

7. How do I demonstrate consistency with my behavior?

8. How do I practice being non-judgmental and open to new approaches to life?

9. How do I cultivate positive relationships in my life and career?

10. How do I create accountability in my life?

11. How do I demonstrate competency in my actions, words, and continual learning?

12. How am I transparent with others and face my flaws, fears, and dreams with myself?

When you look honestly at yourself, do you mostly see negative or positive aspects of your life and how you live it?

What we focus on expands in our minds. We can pour back into our cups or take more away every day. This means we can fill our minds with positive thoughts, behaviors, and beliefs or let negativity and self-doubt drain our mental energy. Having your cup half full isn't just a metaphor; it's a way of operating in your life.

Let's imagine you are continually presented with the same cup daily, which allows you to choose whatever you desire, be it the finest espresso or latte, flavorful and rare tea, fine artisan wine, or whatever you choose for each sip. One caveat: Your actions determine if it runs over or dries up.

Here are the rules: For each thought, behavior, spoken word, or demonstrated belief, your cup results in +/- 1 ounce. This means that every time you engage in a positive action or thought, you add to your mental 'cup, 'while negative actions or thoughts drain it.

Would you rethink your behavior if this were how you approached reward each day?

Eventually, this creates a reinforced habit over time, where no matter what your day presented, you would think, speak, and reactivate your life positively.

What if I told you this is true for you now?

Your mind constantly evaluates your actions. Every positive decision fills your 'mental cup,' releasing dopamine and reinforcing growth. By focusing on positivity, you can rewire your brain to overcome fear.

"Everything you want is on the other side of fear." – Jack Canfield.

Each time you contemplate change, your mind goes through adaptive decision-making patterns. Our prefrontal cortex is responsible for understanding the emotions associated with our decisions, making rational decisions, balancing our thought patterns, and weighing out potential consequences. The challenge lies within which portion of our brain we are tapping into more: the fear zone or the reward center.

Neuroscientific research shows that the prefrontal cortex, responsible for decision-making, regulates the amygdala's fear response, helping us make rational, goal-directed choices. Fear can grip our decision-making process tightly and can be the deterrent to moving forward on our big goals or staying stuck in the worry loop. It is incredibly powerful. It can be used as a motivator or inhibitor.

However, the reward is stronger than fear. Our brain's reward center can create lasting and fortuitous changes. The difference is that fear is always accessible, while reward must be tapped into to create meaningful change.

How do we tap into reward and overcome fear?

To overcome our fears, we must demonstrate to our minds that a particular belief isn't necessary for survival. The only way to do this is to take action. Action catalyzes change, but most of us stay stuck here.

We are waiting for a signal that it's safe to make a move, but the opposite creates change. We must first move by faith to demonstrate that the action was, in fact, valid. By taking action, demonstrating positive change, and reinforcing this through our brain's reward center, we can start rewiring our neural pathways and develop the neuroplasticity required to make bold moves for our future.

This is why we can lean on logic and challenge our beliefs and assumptions. Our assumptions are merely our minds' happy path to perceived success. It doesn't necessarily make it accurate. When we tap into logic, challenge assumptions, and determine what a fallacy is and what is true, we can start to make sense of the voice in our mind, the beliefs we carry, and the hope we can have for the future. It's how we can start to see the saboteurs that hold us back or try to protect us when, in reality, we can ease into letting them go.

Research in Cognitive Behavioral Therapy (CBT) shows that challenging irrational beliefs improves mental well-being and decision-making. We have been developing our beliefs since birth—the first time we fell down when trying to walk, the fear we felt when learning to ride a bike, and the danger of touching a burning flame. Sometimes, we hold onto the fear until we are ready to let it go, either because the motivation to change is so great or because there is irrefutable proof that we can succeed—or both.

Neuroscience has shown that our brains are constantly rewiring themselves through neuroplasticity. Every new habit, every time you challenge your assumptions, you're literally reshaping your brain. As Norman Doidge explains, 'Neurons that fire together, wire together.' When you choose positive actions, you strengthen the neural pathways associated with success, making change easier with each step forward.

Overcoming fear to receive a greater reward.

When my son was younger, he struggled to learn how to ride a bike. I made the mistake of hovering too closely, stifling his confidence. Years later, he decided to try again after seeing all his friends' riding bikes. This time, I stepped back, and he was riding with ease within days. The lesson? Sometimes, we need to let go of fear and trust the process. Success often comes when we least expect it—but only after we've allowed ourselves to fall and get back up.

We hold ourselves back from things we know are possible. There is proof that others have achieved similar results, but we allow our fear to stand in the way. When we can increase our drive and motivation to succeed coupled with reward, we give ourselves an injection of confidence that propels us forward faster than we realize.

The key is in how we start.

We won't succeed the first time we try, but how we view those moments—either as steps toward success or failure—makes the difference.

As Dr. Carol Dweck's research on mindset has shown, people with a growth mindset are more likely to embrace challenges and view failure as an opportunity for growth, essential for building resilience and trust in ourselves.

When we can attach our incremental growth to success, we enable our brain to tap into the reward center, release the stored dopamine, and send us into new waves of increased motivation. This creates the motivational loop of success as opposed to failure. Little by little, we continue to grow, living inside what is known as the Zone of Proximal Development and demonstrating our ability to change, grow, and succeed.

When we try to push ourselves too far, too fast, and expect massive, immediate results, we fall into the lie of failure. We stop short right before we succeed.

For years, my son lacked inner confidence and belief until his motivation to succeed outweighed his fear of failure. All he needed was incremental gains to reinforce his success. At that point, his success rate exponentially increased as he noticed his positive gains and refused to see them as failures.

Here is the beautiful part: We can tap into this portion of our mind whenever we choose. We must decide how we will look at our efforts, speak to ourselves, give credence to, and choose to believe.

This is why continually developing trust with yourself is crucial to your success. It's why positive affirmations, gratitude, and purpose reign supreme when developing habits around your goals and cultivating a relationship with your accomplishments.

Success is a personal contract of accountability to yourself.

If you don't show up for yourself every day, cheer in your corner, speak highly of yourself, or believe in your life's value and worth, then you are breaking that contract. The output dictates the reward, but you must first have faith in yourself, the process, and the belief that you are here for a greater purpose beyond what you can fully perceive.

As Steve Maraboli stated in his book Life, the Truth, and Being Free, "Life doesn't get easier or more forgiving; we get stronger and more resilient."

Five Steps to Building Trust in Yourself

1. Set small, achievable goals: Start with a simple task today and turn it into a daily habit. Consistency is key.

2. Practice self-compassion: Acknowledge mistakes without judgment—failure is part of growth. Use a mantra like "I am learning" to shift your mindset.

3. Take calculated risks: Step outside your comfort zone today. Reflect on the results and celebrate small victories to build confidence.

4. Celebrate wins—big or small: Recognize and reward progress, no matter how small. Acknowledge each step forward.

5. Be consistent: Trust builds over time with steady effort. Keep showing up, even when it's hard, to reinforce your habits.

Fear is like a thick fog surrounding us, making everything unclear and hard to navigate. But trust is the light that cuts through that fog, revealing a path forward. The more we trust ourselves, the clearer the road becomes, and the farther we can go.

The path of personal success.

Having lived a life of repeated challenges, what is perceived as failure can be the stepping stone to your success.

I chose to live a life more significant than the sum of my struggles because I knew that it was more important to use those experiences for the greater good than to stay stuck in permanent despair. It wasn't easy, and it took much self-introspection, facing my fears, and working on my internal belief systems.

This moved me from software engineering to purpose-driven leadership and business coaching. If I wanted my story to matter, I would need to rise even higher than where I was operating.

I had overcome so much already, but there was still more to do.

During my early twenties, I survived a nightmarish relationship filled with drugs, power struggles, and narcissistic insecurities. It subjected me to severe emotional, sexual, and physical abuse, from which I narrowly escaped.

During those darkest days, I barely recognized the person staring back at me in the mirror. I felt hollow as if every ounce of my spirit had been drained away, leaving nothing but fear and doubt. I wondered if I'd ever feel whole again. But I mustered the last bit of strength I had, and I ran for my life out of the dark little house that held me, prisoner, despite all my fears because the alternative—staying one more day—was unthinkable.

For years, I struggled with the lingering fear, shame, and insecurity as I navigated recurring trauma, deep depression, threats from former friends, and the eventual release of my abuser from prison three years later.

In my late twenties, I again experienced incredible trauma. I spent years struggling to understand the symptoms my body faced that impacted my ability to process food. After years of uncertainty, I was finally diagnosed with ulcerative colitis and, a week later, found myself with a ruptured colon and two major surgeries—an ileostomy followed by a j-pouch reconnection. I was devastated after my first surgery, staring at my patched body, thinning head of hair, and sagging skin and bones, wondering why this had happened. My trust had been broken again, this time with the medical system. Facing the overwhelming medical debt from treatments and hospital stays, I struggled with self-confidence, imposter syndrome, and harsh self-criticism.

Despite everything, I kept fighting for my life, my freedom to make my own choices, and a path toward greater fulfillment. In my late twenties, I completed college and collaborated with top military agencies, Fortune 500 companies, and world-class leaders from renowned organizations. My ambitions grew beyond what I imagined, fueled by an increasing passion, purpose, and drive as I watched myself evolve.

I wasn't sure if I would succeed in the ways I envisioned, but I knew what near-death felt like, what it was to be a prisoner, and what it meant to have no control over your own life—and I knew I didn't want that for my future.

"Everything can be taken from a man but one thing: the last of the human freedoms—to choose one's attitude in any given set of circumstances, to choose one's own way."

— Viktor E. Frankl, Man's Search for Meaning

Looking back at the woman who once doubted her every move, I can't help but feel a sense of awe. The person I am today—strong, driven, and purpose-filled—is someone I once thought was unreachable. But she was always there, waiting for me to find her.

A calling for life.

You can break free from fear and rebuild trust in yourself. Every choice you make today can move you closer to your desired life. Don't wait for permission. Don't wait for the 'right' moment. Take the first step now. Trust yourself, embrace change, and let today be the start of your transformation.

Understanding how the mind works has profoundly shaped the way I approach life. As Anne Betz once said, 'Neuroscience is just a 12-letter word for hope."

The future may be uncertain, but we unlock curiosity, confidence, and belief in our potential when we rise above fear. Be bold. Trust yourself. Break free from the patterns holding you back, and step boldly into the life you were meant to live.

***

To contact Jessica:

Website: https://jessicaricecoaching.com

Email: info@jessicaricecoaching

LinkedIn: https://linkedin.com/in/jessicakarlrice

YouTube: https://youtube.com/@jessicaricecoaching

Dr. Yolanda Davis

Dr. (h.c.) Yolanda Davis, a United States Air Force veteran, is a published author, speaker, and real estate investor, including syndication investing.

As a published author, her debut book, *No Satan, Not This Time*, empowers readers to establish a powerful relationship with the word "no," She shares her personal journey of saying no, pivoting, and embracing new opportunities. Her upcoming books, *The Pivot Decision*, shares how you can choose the decision that causes the trajectory of your life to change, and *A Pivot Woman*, tells the inspiring story of two friends who strategically pivoted to achieve their desired outcomes for fulfillment and happiness in their lives. Her third book, *The F in Your Finances*, introduces a unique approach to financial literacy emphasizing the importance of "finding, fueling, and funding" one's financial life. Yolanda has also contributed to several anthologies.

Yolanda is a speaker who has addressed diverse audiences at churches, schools, and private organizations. She has received numerous accolades, including the 2022 President's Lifetime Achievement Award and an Honorary Doctorate in Humanitarianism for her pivotal roles in providing housing for homeless individuals. Her leadership roles include serving as Commander and Vice Commander for military organizations, Executive director for a non-profit and Vice President for civic organizations. She offers innovative strategies and practical solutions that drive meaningful transformation with the goal of authenticity and freedom.

Introduction: The Power of the Pivot Decision

By Yolanda Davis

This introduction frames pivoting as a positive, proactive step and invites readers to see change as an opportunity for growth and alignment with their true desires.

The need to pivot isn't necessarily a sign of failure but can be a testament to being tuned in to your life so much that you know that you must shift your actions to change your regular projected outcome. You understand that you are the author of your life, and you can shift your choices and direction to have a different experience and outcome.

Pivoting isn't always born out of a necessity due to difficult circumstances. Sometimes, it can be fueled by your innate desire to grow and expand yourself to fulfill your goals and desires. Resonating with this after my divorce, I realized that I needed to stretch far beyond my comfort zone mentally, physically, financially, socially, and emotionally. I chose to return to school to further my education, immersed myself in self-development courses, and developed new skill sets that contributed to me creating a life new life.

My life is a testament to the need to pivot across multiple areas, and I have learned firsthand how important it is to adapt, shift, and adjust to many things that have come my way. Far too often, the need to change direction comes from unwanted and unexpected circumstances. Each pivot was a step towards personal growth and experiencing myself as a new version of myself.

The *Pivot Decision* for me emerged from the realization that my marriage of 27 years had ended and that I was going to need a new identity. I'll admit, after my divorce, I was terrified about what my life was going to look like; after all, my primary role was a stay-at-home mom. Although I had managed real estate investments and business and held part-time jobs, I never felt like I had a trailblazing career, especially after nearly a decade of service in the United States Air Force. My contributions, though impactful in their own way, weren't the kind that society typically acknowledges or celebrates. This left me feeling somewhat disempowered and uncertain about my future.

I learned that every skill I had learned—from investing to managing family real estate, starting and overseeing a transitional home, partnering with local agencies, coordinating fundraisers, and engaging deeply with my community with my dedication to personal development—would serve as a catalyst for my courage and confidence to pivot into new and uncharted territories.

My time in the military instilled the values of resilience, adaptability, and a mission-driven mindset. These qualities, along with my experience as a homemaker, businesswoman, and community leader, were invaluable assets to support me as I navigated this new phase of my life; it was time to overcome my fears, redefine my path, and transform my life.

THE PIVOT DECISION TO LEARN

Learning is the foundation upon which all personal growth and transformation is built and is not limited to the classroom or traditional education. In the journey of life, we can pivot and learn from all the situations that we encounter, whether failure, success, or untimely challenges. Pivoting to learn means that you allow yourself to be open to receiving new information, perspectives, and new experiences. When we pivot to learn, we let go of the fact that our way is not the only way and open ourselves up to new possibilities.

I immersed myself in the world of personal development and surrounded myself with leaders and mentors from whom I could learn and grow. I focused on developing and shifting my mindset and inner self and committed 30 hours a week or more to self-improvement. I took the process of mental evolution seriously, engaged deeply, and continuous learning. I kept an open mind, embraced my new teachings, and felt stronger and more courageous. Every step in my learning propelled me forward and brought me increased clarity and self-awareness. I began to lead my life with an unstoppable energy and was able to step into leadership to support others in achieving their personal development goals. This experience was life-changing and solidified my commitment to lifelong learning and positioned me as a committed leader, team player, and lifelong learner.

THE PIVOT DECISION TO LISTEN

It is said that listening is one of the most powerful yet underutilized skills in communication, leadership, and personal growth. I began listening to positive affirmations, motivational speeches, podcasts, audiobooks, or talks from thought leaders like Tony Robbins, Les Brown, Joe Miguel, Lisa Nicholas, Dr. Joe Dispenza, and spiritual leaders like Eckhart Tolle or Deepak Chopra, whose insights on mindfulness, presence, and connection to a higher purpose had a huge impact on my life.

Listening to inspirational and motivational talks daily allowed me to absorb content that promoted optimism and a mindset of abundance, reshaping many of my beliefs and even shifting many of my thinking patterns toward success.

I took communications courses to develop my listening skills and practice reducing my desire to always speak. I had to learn how to be fully present to hear what others were saying. I learned that listening is more than just waiting for your turn to speak; it requires active engagement and your full attention to the person you are communicating with. By listening with the intention of being present, I was able to capture the views and perspectives of the other person.

I began to pay attention and listen to my internal dialogue. It felt like I had an ongoing recording playing in my head from the motivational and inspirational recordings that I listened to daily. I felt as if my spirit was yearning to stay highly motivated and resilient to achieve emotional, physical, spiritual, social, and financial success. During this time, I developed a love for Indian flute music, meditation, sound bowls, nature sounds, binaural beats, and uplifting music to help align my energy with a sense of peace and calm.

I put myself on a schedule because of my love for R&B and Old School music. I ensured that I listened to more high-frequency music because I felt calmer, connected, and in alignment spiritually.

THE PIVOT DECISION TO LET GO

As I evolved in my life, it seemed natural for me to begin to let go—of some people, places, situations, circumstances, beliefs, and even parts of myself that no longer served me. Letting go was not easy because I wanted to hold on to my position of being right, and at times, I even wanted to be the victim. The problem with wanting to be right only led me to feeling stuck and not moving forward. Letting go became crucial for me to move on and find some peace. Pivoting to let go is one of the most powerful decisions we can make in life, and it begins with our physical well-being. When we hold on to what no longer serves us, whether it's a job, a relationship, or a habit, we carry unnecessary stress that takes a toll on our bodies. I've learned that letting go is not a sign of weakness but an act of self-love. By pivoting away from the things that deplete our energy, we give our bodies the rest, nourishment, and care they need to thrive. This shift frees up the space for movement, growth, and healing, allowing us to become stronger and more vibrant versions of ourselves.

Mentally, pivoting to let go opens the door to clarity and peace. I know how easy it is to get trapped in a cycle of overthinking, replaying old conversations, and holding on to outdated beliefs that no longer align with who I am today. By choosing to let go, I clear away the mental clutter that clouds my judgment and hinders my ability to see new possibilities. It's like clearing the fog from my mind, allowing me to focus on the present and set new goals. Pivoting is about creating a mental space where new ideas, solutions, and creativity can flourish without being overshadowed by the past.

Emotionally, letting go is a courageous act of healing. I've experienced firsthand the emotional weight of holding on to pain, resentment, or regret. It can be hard to release emotions that feel so deeply rooted, but I've come to realize that holding on to them only prolongs the hurt. Pivoting allows me to step into emotional freedom by embracing forgiveness—both for myself and others. It's not about forgetting or ignoring what happened but rather about releasing its emotional grip on me. This decision empowers me to reclaim my emotional energy and invest it in relationships and experiences that bring me joy and fulfillment.

Socially, the power of pivoting to let go is transformative. I've found that not everyone or everything will grow with me as I grow—and that's okay. It's important to let go of relationships that no longer align with my values, dreams, or vision for the future. While this can be difficult, it creates room for new, supportive, and inspiring connections to enter my life. Letting go socially allows me to surround myself with people who uplift and challenge me in positive ways. It's a beautiful process of shedding the old and embracing the new, creating a social environment that fosters growth, connection, and shared purpose

THE PIVOT DECISION TO LEAD

Now that I had let go of so much, I began resonating with my abilities to lead myself first and then others. I had learned a lot over ten years, and it was time for me to step up and lead boldly and powerfully. The first person that I had to learn to lead effectively was myself. I began to lead myself out of my quagmire and take responsibility for being the leader of my life. Pivoting to lead myself was daunting and even very confrontational at times because I needed to become self-aware, understand my strengths and weaknesses, and cultivate the discipline needed and necessary to move forward with my goals.

Once I mastered leading myself, the next step was for me to lead others. Leading others means demonstrating the values and behaviors to inspire. It requires vulnerability and transparency because people are more likely to follow authentic and relatable leaders. I was willing to admit my mistakes, learn from them, and show others that growth is a continuous journey. Pivoting to lead others also meant recognizing that leadership is not about the leader—it is also about the people that the leader leads.

THE PIVOT DECISION TO LAUGH

It is said that laughter is good for the soul, yet I didn't have enough of it in my life at the time. I began to treat laughing as if it were my daily vitamin. Soon, many of my friends noticed my silly and funny side. Laughing intentionally shifted my perspective, relieved some of my burdens, and contributed to my healing. I have faced moments when my challenges seemed overwhelming, yet in these periods, I learned the transformative power of laughter.

I realized that laughter isn't just a reaction to humor; it's a choice we make when we decide to seek out the lighter side of life, even when things seem dark. There's a difference between avoiding life's difficulties and using humor to navigate through them. One of the most profound lessons I've learned is that laughter creates space between me and my problems. When I laugh, I'm no longer consumed by the issue at hand—I'm able to take a step back, breathe, and see things from a broader perspective. It helps me realize that this, too, shall pass. I remember times when I felt overwhelmed, and the mere act of laughing broke the tension in the room or my heart, helping me reset and approach things with more clarity.

Pivoting to laughter doesn't mean dismissing pain or ignoring challenges. It's about embracing a balanced approach to life. Laughter gives us the resilience to face hardship while also celebrating life's joys. It can remind me to be present, to appreciate moments of levity, and to know that laughter can coexist with growth, healing, and even sadness.

In learning to pivot toward laughter, I've also discovered that it's contagious. When I laugh, others around me tend to laugh, too, and the energy of the room shifts. It's a gift we give to ourselves and to others, a shared experience that connects us in joy. Ultimately, pivoting to laughter has been one of the most freeing choices I've made, and I continue to prioritize it as a necessary and powerful part of my life.

THE PIVOT DECISION TO LOVE

My journey of love began with self-love, and I've come to understand that this pivotal shift starts with me fully accepting myself—flaws, strengths, and everything in between. For me, self-love means that I treat myself with kindness, compassion, and respect. It's about recognizing my own self-worth without relying on external validation and learning to find fulfillment from within. This pivot to self-love is essential because I've realized that I can't genuinely love others until I first learn to love myself.

Self-love has become the foundation for healthier relationships in my life. When I prioritize loving myself, I gain the power to set boundaries that protect my well-being, communicate my needs clearly, and show up authentically in all areas of my life; I honor the unique person I am. The more I embrace who I am, the more I can contribute to the well-being of others from a place of true compassion and empathy. Loving others means seeing them for who they are—without judgment or expectations. I've learned that offering support, understanding, and compassion starts by recognizing humanity in others, just as I've learned to recognize it in myself. This perspective has deepened my relationships and strengthened my connections with those around me.

The love I give to others reflects the love I've cultivated within myself and reminds me of how interconnected we all are. When I approach relationships from a place of love, I'm better equipped to navigate challenges, communicate with kindness, and offer support without losing myself in the process. I can embrace the diversity of perspectives and experiences that others bring into my life, fostering a sense of unity and understanding.

By making these pivots—first to self-love and then to loving others—I feel that I am contributing to a more loving and compassionate world. I've discovered that love is not only about romantic relationships or grand gestures; it's about the small, consistent actions that nurture and sustain the people we care about.

Ultimately, my journey has taught me that self-love is not a destination but a continuous process. It requires daily practice and patience, but the rewards are invaluable to me and others. As I continue to embrace this path, I find peace, joy, and fulfillment in my relationship with myself and others.

THE PIVOT DECISION TO LIVE-LOUDLY

This chapter boldly summarizes all my previous chapters and expresses the overall impact of how I was willing to be, open pivot regularly, and its impact on the quality of my life. When I talk about living loudly, I am not talking about the volume of your voice; I am talking about the volume of the presence of your essence. I am saying that because I was choosing alignment for my life, I felt I was being changed at my core. People would say they could feel my spirit, energy, and even the essence of who I was being. Now, I am not saying that I am done; however, this is just my acknowledgment that a few things have shifted, and the outcome has been rewarding.

Placing myself in environments where I could listen to great leaders was crucial for my new beginnings and transformation. I could have walked out of any of those life-changing courses, and my life would have been just fine, yet I didn't, and I am grateful that I chose to be resilient, relentless, and even unstoppable after staking a claim to my "pivot decision." I am glad I listened to my inner voice and some of the greatest and most profound leaders.

I've developed my new identity, embraced my authentic voice, and lived loudly in essence. I have established new relationships all over the world, and new doors and many opportunities have allowed me to expand in the business world.

I believe I am living loud because I am authentic and aligned with my calling. This pivot is about embracing my uniqueness, unapologetically expressing who I am, and living a life that reflects my deepest passions and values. Living out loud doesn't mean being the loudest voice in the room; it means living with purpose, clarity, and authenticity. It's about making choices that connect with my soul and light me up, and I can influence others because of this.

When I pivot to live loud, in my essence, I am in my power. I choose to no longer play small or hide parts of myself. Instead, I walk in my true essence and allow it to guide me toward the life I'm meant to live. My journey of pivoting honors my growth and encourages me to share my gifts with the world. By living authentically, I free myself and inspire others to do the same; there is a rippling effect of empowerment

As I make pivotal decisions about learning, listening, letting go, leading, laughing, loving, and living loudly, I become the fullest expression of who I am at my core. I embrace my growth, truth, and transformation, moving through life with purpose, resiliency, clarity, boldness, and loudness. This is how I become and experience the truest version of myself.

Melissa Barnes

Melissa is a dedicated wife, a proud momma of three fantastic children, and a passionate career woman. Together, they live a very full and rewarding lifestyle that has them running every moment of every day, from school to work to hockey, dance, swimming, and gymnastics. Their days are full of hustle and bustle.

After two decades in the death and grief care industry, running a business of high demand and emotions, as well as her family life, she realized that she needed to make a change when her drinking habits began to interfere with her relationships, well-being, and self-confidence. In other words, alcohol was draining more than it was adding. So, she started writing a "contract for change" with herself and entered into a transformative journey of empowered alcohol-free living.

Nearly four years later, as an Alcohol-Free Life Coach and Empowerment Coach, Melissa helps moms break free from the grip of alcohol and step into their true potential. Her values are built on a foundation of empathy, experience, and empowerment, and she is dedicated to supporting women as they reclaim their lives and embrace their roles as powerful mothers, professionals, and individuals.

Melissa flips the script on sobriety, breaking the stigma around women and drinking and inspiring other women to embrace an alcohol-free life full of strength, purpose, and joy. She aims to empower women to rediscover themselves, rebuild their confidence, and thrive in every aspect of their lives.

Reclaiming My Life, Rewriting My Story! A Journey to An Empowered Alcohol-Free Life

Melissa Barnes, Certified AF Life Coach & NLP Practitioner

My story with alcohol started like many others - young, carefree, and full of life. Drinking was just part of the experience: at parties, socializing, or traveling. I enjoyed it until one day, years later, I realized I was drinking too much. What had once been occasional fun began to creep into my life more frequently, and before I knew it, I was drinking too often, lying about it, and eventually, to the point of blacking out.

As the years went by, alcohol became ingrained in my social circle, a habit that escalated beyond "just a few." Parties went on all weekend; camping involved several cases and bottles, and trips were planned around drinking, pub crawls, nightclubs, bonfires—everything was a party. If you're reading this nodding your head like you understand, you'll also understand that these parties didn't always end well!

Years passed, and alcohol was simply part of my routine. If you've ever lived this way, you know exactly how messy these all-weekend parties can get. But at the time, it felt normal. The only people who dared question my drinking were my parents. My father once told me, "You drink like a trucker." No disrespect to truckers - his point was that I, a 120-pound, intelligent, athletic woman, could out-drink most men.

Despite this, I was what people would call "high functioning." I attended college, graduated with honors, held a steady job, and supported myself. By all appearances, I was thriving. But something was quietly brewing just beneath the surface.

In 2009, my health took a turn when I was diagnosed with Graves' disease, an autoimmune disorder that wreaked havoc on my body. My blood pressure was dangerously high, I experienced intense muscle spasms, tremors, bulging eyes, and blurred vision, and I was constantly exhausted. After years of battling symptoms and standard treatments weren't working, I was encouraged by my specialist to have surgery to remove my thyroid gland completely.

The symptoms started to improve almost immediately (except for my eyes). But you know what else changed? My tolerance to alcohol. I could no longer drink you under the table, blackouts were becoming more & more usual, daily drinking to overcome 'hang-xiety' was normal, becoming "that drunk girl" ~ wait, what? What happened to me?? Once I had my surgery and my metabolism and systems started to return to a normal and steady state, my tolerance to alcohol also changed, and so did my relationship with alcohol.

When I met my now-husband, I could still have an amazing night out, but the following days were rough. I found myself reaching for alcohol not for pleasure but to numb the symptoms of my hangovers. It was a vicious cycle.

Motherhood brought on new challenges. The overwhelm became palpable with one, two, then three children, each with their own needs and schedules. I was a full-time working mom, running a business, managing the household, and constantly on the go ~ hockey, swimming, dance, gymnastics, soccer—you name it. The demands left me searching for a release, something to relax me, and once again, I turned to alcohol.

Yet, the more I drank, the more I lost myself. I detached from the people I loved and the life I had built. I knew something had to change. The moment came after one particularly rough night. I looked in the mirror and saw someone I barely recognized—tired, worn out, and lost. That's when I decided to reclaim my life.

Past attempts of cutting out alcohol using traditional methods did not work for me. I had tried, but it did not resonate with me. So, I crafted a plan using skills I'd developed during my 20-year career in the grief care industry. I wrote a contract to myself, a vow to release alcohol from my life. I signed it, dated it, and committed to never looking back. This wasn't just about quitting drinking; it was about stepping into my power and becoming the woman I knew I could be.

This wasn't just a decision; it was a transformation. I dove into the work, developing strategies rooted in empowerment, neurolinguistic programming (NLP), and personal growth. I realized I didn't need anything outside of myself to thrive. I already had everything I needed to be the best mom, wife, daughter, entrepreneur, and human being I could be.

My journey to sobriety wasn't about abstaining from alcohol alone; it was about breaking free from addiction in my mind. It was about rewiring my relationship with alcohol, changing the way I thought about it, and empowering myself to live fully. I was done hiding behind excuses or seeking temporary escapes. I was ready to take control.

Three-and-a-half years ago, I made a promise to myself, and I've kept it every single day since. It wasn't always easy. There were challenges along the way, but I never gave in to the urge to drink. I stayed committed because I knew what was at stake - my life, my family, my dreams.

Through this journey, I've discovered a profound truth: **we are not powerless**. We are capable of breaking free from addiction and rebuilding our lives, no matter how deep we've sunk. We can thrive in our sober lives and do it on our own terms. We can attend parties, concerts, and social events without a second thought about drinking. We are not defined by alcohol or addiction. We are so much more.

Women, especially mothers, face immense pressure in today's world. The demands placed on us are overwhelming, and sometimes, alcohol seems like the easiest way to cope. But I'm here to tell you - there's a much better way. You don't need alcohol to relax, to fit in, or to feel whole. You already have everything you need within you to live a vibrant, fulfilling life.

The process of healing begins by understanding the subconscious mind. Everything we do is influenced by it—the habits we form, the routines we follow, and the coping mechanisms we develop. Drinking becomes ingrained in our subconscious as a response to certain emotions or situations, whether it's to numb the pain of grief, relieve stress, or simply "have fun." But once we recognize these patterns, we can break free from them. We can rewire our minds and create healthy and empowering habits.

You see, the subconscious manifests everything we do. Consider the subconscious a storage unit of memories, learnings, thoughts, and routines that have stored away everything you've ever done. Simply put, if you've developed an unhealthy habit of daily, binge, or heavy regular drinking, these routines/habits/triggers are presented by the subconscious and feed our conscious mind to put it into action!

Let me explain a little more; I will use grief as an example. Whether someone has passed away or you are going through a divorce, this is a highly emotionally charged state where we feel a surge of uncontrollable emotions ranging from heartbreak, hopelessness, and even anger. If we have chosen to drink alcohol to "drown" these feelings and numb them out, we've attached in our subconscious the feeling of sadness, hopelessness, despair, and even anger to the act of drinking as a coping mechanism! What does this mean? It means that as you travel along in life, each time you feel these strong emotions, where does your mind go? To the drink!

Our subconscious mind is the powerhouse creating everything happening in your life; it will manifest from deep-rooted beliefs (positive or negative). It's crucial to develop a healthy relationship with your subconscious & conscious mind and understand how our minds work. If you find yourself repeating behavior that is no longer serving you positively and feel these actions or behaviors are uncontrollable, it might be time to go deeper and discover what is lying under the surface of those thoughts. This profound work truly is the foundation for this system; this will build a solid, healthy foundation. It is a forward-thinking program, relatable for today and the future; this is leading the way to a beautiful, fulfilling life, freeing yourself from alcohol dependency for good!

It's about healing from the inside out. It's about rewiring your thoughts, rebuilding your relationship with yourself, and stepping into a life of true freedom. I've used these techniques to build my own alcohol-free life, and now I'm sharing them with other women who want to reclaim their power. Today, I live a life free from alcohol, and I've never looked back. I no longer feel the pull of addiction. I socialize without issue, and I've built a life that I love, a life that is fulfilling, purposeful, and filled with joy. I don't need alcohol in my life, and neither do you.

When we make the decision to release alcohol from our lives, the first thing we notice is a dramatic shift in our clarity. It's as if a fog lifts, and we begin to see the world around us and within us with new eyes. In the early stages of sobriety, this clarity is subtle, but over time, it becomes a powerful tool that allows us to tap into a deeper understanding of ourselves and our surroundings. We begin to discover new layers of potential and opportunity that were previously hidden by the haze of alcohol. One of the most significant transformations happens in our relationships. As we free ourselves from alcohol's grip, we begin to rebuild and strengthen the connections that matter most. Our relationships with our spouses, children, and ourselves evolve in ways that are often profound and unexpected.

For many, alcohol can serve as a barrier in relationships, distancing us from our partners in subtle ways. It may numb us from emotional intimacy or cause communication breakdowns, as alcohol can become the default mechanism for coping with stress or avoiding conflict. Releasing alcohol allows us to reconnect with our spouses on a deeper level. Without alcohol clouding our emotions, we are more present and available for honest and vulnerable communication. We become better listeners, more attuned to our partner's needs, and more capable of expressing our feelings clearly. The absence of alcohol also means the absence of unnecessary arguments or misunderstandings fueled by intoxication. This creates space for healing, rebuilding trust, and re-establishing intimacy.

One of the most beautiful gifts of an alcohol-free life is the opportunity to show up fully for your children. Alcohol, whether we realize it or not, can rob us of precious moments with them. Whether it's through missed opportunities to connect or our emotional unavailability when under the influence, alcohol can create distance between us and the ones who need us most. After releasing alcohol, I found myself able to engage more deeply with my children. I became more patient, more present, and more connected to their emotional needs. I no longer turned to alcohol to unwind after a long day of parenting; instead, I sought more mindful and intentional ways to bond with them. I was able to cultivate a more loving and supportive relationship with my children. Children are incredibly intuitive and can sense when we are fully present. By showing up as our most authentic selves, we model emotional resilience, self-awareness, and healthy coping mechanisms. We become the example of the kind of clarity, strength, and inner peace we want our children to carry with them into their own lives. This is one of the most powerful legacies we can leave with them.

One of the greatest revelations in sobriety is the realization that the power to create the life we want has been within us all along. Alcohol can dull this awareness, leading us to feel stuck or powerless in certain areas of our lives. But when we strip away the layers of alcohol-induced brain fog, we reconnect with our true potential. The mind is a powerful tool, and once we tap into its total capacity, we can create a life of abundance, clarity, and fulfillment. This process begins by retraining our thought patterns and breaking free from limiting beliefs. Alcohol often reinforces negative thought loops, convincing us that we are not enough, that our past mistakes bind us, or that we need something outside of ourselves to cope with life's challenges. In sobriety, we have the clarity to challenge these beliefs and rewrite our internal narrative. This shift in mindset can have a ripple effect on all areas of life. We become more intentional about the decisions we make, the opportunities we pursue, and the relationships we cultivate. We start believing that we can achieve our goals and dreams and take empowered steps toward creating the life we truly desire. For me, this meant revisiting my career and passions. I tapped into the skills and experiences I had accumulated over the years and channeled them into new ventures. The clarity I gained in sobriety allowed me to see where I had been holding myself back and gave me the courage to pursue opportunities that aligned with my values and vision. This, in turn, created a sense of abundance, not just in terms of material success but emotional and spiritual beauty.

One of the keys to maintaining this sense of abundance and clarity is through mindfulness. Living sober requires us to be fully present in each moment, and mindfulness helps us cultivate this presence. Through practices such as meditation, journaling, or simply taking time to reflect, we can deepen our connection to ourselves and the world around us. Mindfulness also helps us maintain a sense of gratitude. In sobriety, it's easy to focus on what we've "lost" or "given up," but mindfulness reminds us of all we have gained. It shifts our focus from scarcity to abundance, helping us appreciate life's simple joys, whether it's a peaceful moment with our family, a new career opportunity, or the clarity we experience in our day-to-day lives.

As we continue to live alcohol-free, we begin to see the impact it has on our relationships, our mindset, and our sense of awareness. We become more present, more intentional, and more connected to the people and experiences that matter most. Releasing alcohol is not just about removing something negative from our lives; it's about making space for something bigger. It's about stepping into our full potential, creating a life of clarity and abundance, and becoming the best version of ourselves for our spouses, our children, and ourselves. Reflecting on my journey, I realize that this transformation is not as simple as sobriety; it's about empowerment. It's about reclaiming our power, rewriting our story, and embracing the limitless possibilities that come with living a life of clarity and purpose.

This year, I felt called to share my story and help other women, mothers, professionals, and women just like me who are struggling with their relationship with alcohol. I saw women stuck where I once was, unsure of how to break free. I vowed to change the way women viewed alcohol addiction and help them find a path to freedom in the modern world.

Through this work, you will understand and believe you are not powerless. We are capable of breaking free from the chains of alcohol and rebuilding our lives from the inside out. We can change our lives the moment we change our minds, and we can do it in the privacy of our own homes, creating lifelong strength that carries us forward. Life does not need to stop; we can still attend parties, concerts, and sporting events without giving alcohol a second thought. We don't need alcohol to have fun, to socialize, or to feel whole. We are enough, just as we are.

To the woman reading this who feels like she's at a crossroads, I want you to know that I believe in you. I know you have the strength and the power to overcome this obstacle. You deserve the best life has to offer, as do your children and loved ones. I understand that the idea of giving up alcohol might feel scary. You might wonder how you'll manage social situations or whether you'll lose friends. You might fear being judged or feeling isolated. But I promise you, on the other side of alcohol is a life more fulfilling than you can imagine.

I have never regretted making this shift in my life. I've only gained peace of mind, clarity, and a deep sense of gratitude. You can have this too. You are not alone; you have everything within you to create the life of your dreams.

I do not identify as an alcoholic, and I don't define myself by my past. I'm simply a woman who has chosen to live a full, empowered, alcohol-free life, and I want that for you.

You deserve to live the life of your dreams. Be the best version of yourself for your children, your family, and most importantly, for you.

You can create a life you love, **LIVE WITH PURPOSE**, and start right now.

***

To contact Melissa:

Web: Www.sobrietycoachmelissa.com

Email: Melissa@sobrietycoachmelissa.com

IG: @Melissa.barnes.771/

FB: https://www.facebook.com/melissa.barnes.771?mibextid=LQQJ4d

Other: https://sobrietycoachmelissa.ck.page/e730587098

Jennifer Wallace

Jennifer Wallace, also known as Coach Jennifer W, is a dedicated coach with a mission to empower and build high-achieving professionals, especially women in high-stress careers. Her journey is a testament to resilience and transformation, having overcome an emotionally abusive marriage that left her homeless and broken, toxic, and narcissistic relationships, the profound grief of losing two children, and the challenges of a stressful work environment paired with health diagnoses.

Despite these adversities, Jennifer has strived and thrived. She rebuilt her self-worth, reclaimed her emotional independence, and restored her individual power. Today, as a mindfulness and transformational coach, Jennifer is passionate about sharing her story and using her experiences as a lifeline for women who feel unworthy and struggle to heal from toxic relationships.

Jennifer coaches with a purpose, empowering women with the tools they need to maintain their power, create healthier relationships, and ultimately live happier, more fulfilling lives. Her personal and professional journey fuels her commitment to helping others navigate their paths toward healing and empowerment.

From Toxic Relationships to Empowered Living: Blueprint to an Empowered Resilient Life

By Jennifer Wallace

"Out of suffering have emerged the strongest souls; the most massive characters are seared with scars."- Khalil Gibran.

I remember vividly, I was about seven or eight years old when my mother decided to end her abusive relationship with my stepfather. He was a man whose physical and verbal abuse had left a long-lasting, scary mark on our lives. I recall an instance when I required help finishing my math homework after school and would get chastised and smacked on the head if I didn't get it right.

I can remember seeing my mother filled with anger in her eyes as she gathered the courage and strength to leave him, taking my sister and me with nothing but the clothes on our backs. We found refuge in a shelter in New Mexico, a temporary haven that shielded us from the immediate danger. Despite the uncertainty, my mother's determination to return to our home in Colorado had made it through. Her bravery and quick action in the face of adversity were remarkable, and they planted the first seeds of resilience within me.

Her actions taught me a powerful lesson: that the first step toward a better life often begins with the courage to walk away from what no longer serves you. Watching her navigate those horrible times, I learned that resilience is not born from comfort but from the trials and tribulations that test our strength and willpower. This early experience of witnessing my mother reclaim her life from the grips of abuse became the bedrock of my journey toward empowerment and self-worth. This would later be the influence and drive of how I became independent and self-reliant.

Experiences with Toxic Relationships

"I am not what happened to me, I am what I choose to become." – Carl Jung.

The first time I experienced a toxic relationship was when I was married. The marriage was emotionally and mentally abusive. I found myself homeless and had to start over from scratch. Not knowing how to set boundaries and watch out for the signs, the years that followed I would end up another toxic relationship. This relationship would result in me dealing with a narcissistic person that would leave me depressed, stressed, and with health issues. This time, with the heartbreak of losing two children. All while dealing with a toxic work environment. Lastly, another relationship where later on in the relationship I found myself dealing with an emotionally unavailable, narcissistic partner who would dismiss, devalue, neglect, and disrespect me. I decided to get out of that relationship as quickly as possible and left. I would also find this to lead me down the path of another health diagnosis of PTSD.

In my professional journey, there was a time when I faced a toxic work environment that felt suffocating, with my contributions being overlooked or claimed by others. There were instances where the ideas I introduced were misappropriated, and misinformation about my actions was circulated, creating a distorted narrative that spread through the workplace. This led to feelings of isolation as I was excluded from team activities and faced an atmosphere filled with untruths and misconceptions. The toxicity of the environment was overwhelming, making it a constant challenge to maintain my focus and integrity amidst the adversity. This took a toll on me emotionally, mentally, and physically, yet that position was unexpectedly shutting down. A moment others dreaded. I found a sense of peace knowing it was coming to an end and knowing it was God, or what some may call a divine intervention, that would lead me to a new path where I would flourish and ascend through the ranks in a new career. This would be my opportunity to exit that toxic work environment.

I would like to take a moment and ask you to journal and reflect on your own experiences with toxic relationships. Take a moment to journal about a time you felt undervalued. What were the signs you might have missed? How did it make you feel?

This was my breaking point, and I began to grow tired of feeling unworthy, not having solid boundaries, and wanting to feel happy again. At that moment, I decided to be cherished, loved, and celebrated, not tolerated. I started to learn that if I wanted to be happy, these were the things I needed to improve on to begin the healing process. This is where I say this was the part of the "fight" healing process started.

Think about a realization moment when you decided enough is enough. What triggered this decision, and how did you feel afterwards?

Reclaiming Myself, Where Transformation and Empowerment Began

"You are worthy of love and respect. You have the power to reclaim your life. - Unknown"

Along my journey, I took steps to reclaim myself. I created these steps for what I now call "Fight, Reclaim, and Restore." The fight means (which was my toxic experience I explained earlier) the ongoing struggle to get back to yourself after being in a toxic relationship. The reclaim part means starting the path to healing or the healing process. Lastly, the restore part means rebuilding oneself to become the best version of yourself and living a fulfilling, empowered life.

The steps included rediscovering who I was and finding my self-worth again, being around positive atmospheres and others, and reaching out for support. I began practicing mindfulness and meditation. Mindfulness is a type of meditation that focuses on being intensely aware of what you're sensing and feeling in the moment without judgment or interpretation. This helped me cope with stressful situations at work or anytime I again started to feel those damaged emotions that came from being in toxic relationships. It helped me to get back on track and remember that I am no longer in that situation and that I am here in the present and safe and no longer in that stressful environment.

Do you practice mindfulness? How has it helped you and transformed your mindset?

I created steps to reclaim my self-worth by first Letting go of the past. I learned how to forgive myself and those individuals who caused the hurt. I did this by journaling my feelings and emotions. I released my hurt and anger by speaking in prayer. This helped me say the words so my mind could let go. I found positive activities. I created what I call a "Joy list." I listed all the things that I could possibly do at that moment that would make me happy. I held myself accountable for doing those things on the list and did them. I would schedule reminders on my phone to go off at a certain time of the day so I can make sure I did that specific activity. This list brought joy to me and took my mind off of negative thoughts and emotions. Lastly, I used positive affirmations that I would save on my mobile phone and look at daily or when I was in a mood to uplift me and program my mind to stay positive. These things brought me to create healthy habits for myself.

The Climb to Empowerment

"Empowerment is not the light at the end of the tunnel but the strength you find as you navigate the darkness. It's the climb where every step you take, no matter how small, brings you closer to the peak of your potential." – Unknown.

I understand the struggle and hard work it takes to get back to a point where you feel like yourself again and like the strong, resilient person you once were. My climb to empowerment meant that I would get back to this place no matter how and what I had to do. It was the mindset that I had to keep pushing and going no matter what. I had experienced financial difficulty, low self-esteem, and feeling lost, and I was determined to get back. I worked long hours and immersed myself in personal empowerment and development. I became better at conversations and relationships with others by having a positive attitude and not letting others who resembled toxic signs or attitudes back into my world. I noticed the health issues I had started to improve and get better. I interviewed in my career and didn't stop till I was promoted. My consistency and perseverance would lead me to become a senior lead in my career in the insurance industry. I learned how to turn my personal recovery into professional growth. Through this transformation, I realized that my worth didn't need external validation. I set boundaries, claimed credit for my ideas, and started asserting my value. Today, I stand before you transformed. I've mastered the art of maintaining balance, protecting my peace with firm boundaries, and creating my narrative in professional environments where respect and integrity prevail. This journey from toxic relationships to resilience and empowered living is not just my story—it's a path many can walk with the right tools and mindset!

Now, I would like you to imagine a situation at work where you need to set a boundary. Write down or journal how you would approach the conversation.

Empowerment Through Coaching

"The best way to find yourself is to lose yourself in the service of others" – Mahatma Gandhi.

The journey I lived and walked through has led me to entrepreneurship to help other women who may be facing the same adversity I've been through. My mission is to help empower professional women, especially those in high-stress careers, such as healthcare, technical, entrepreneurs, and executives, to heal and transform their lives by providing personalized coaching programs encouraging emotional recovery, self-discovery, and lasting empowerment. I find joy in helping women find themselves again, regaining their self-worth, and leading to a happy and fulfilled life. Helping women aligns with my life purpose: to help guide women to healing from toxicity and living a fulfilled life. I live by these core values: integrity, perseverance, self-determination, adaptability, and empathy. I also use these in my coaching teachings as well.

Reflect on the fulfillment you get from helping others and how it aligns with your work purpose. What does this look like in your life?

Actionable Blueprint for Empowered Living

I want to share with you five actionable steps you can take right now to start living an empowered Life.

- **Recognizing the toxic behaviors and learning how to let go.**

Often, when we get ready to experience a toxic relationship, we are just going with our feelings and how we feel and not really being mindful of the behaviors that we see. We often make excuses for bad behavior and brush it off. Before you know it, this will happen so suddenly; the behavior turns into something disrespectful, demeaning, and manipulating. We have to acknowledge these behaviors head-on, address them, and set boundaries. If those boundaries and limits are crossed, we must learn when and how to walk away immediately or as soon as possible. Leaving and dealing with this type of behavior will only grow on you and eat away like poison, leaving you trying to resuscitate your life and your mental and physical well-being. Learning to let go requires you to cut off, get away, and block anyone not acting in your best interest.

What are three things from your past relationships that you need to let go of to move forward?

- **Setting Healthy Boundaries**

This one is the most significant. It will set the stage for you and help you with keeping your confidence, self-worth, and mental stability. Setting healthy boundaries shows respect for yourself and allows you to speak up for yourself and show others how you should be treated. This will lead to being celebrated and not just being tolerated. An example would be someone who keeps dismissing you in conversations to make you feel like you are not important. Also, in your work career, when your boss keeps making you stay late to work on a project. You have to speak up for yourself and be firm in what you say and how you feel about working late.

- **Rebuilding Self-worth**

This step will help you rebuild self-esteem, rediscover love for yourself, and find yourself again. Feeding your mind with positive thoughts and affirmations and being around empowering and happy people will give you a sense of purpose again.

- **Creating Resilience for yourself**

Cognitive reframing is used to replace negative thoughts with positive ones. Try asking yourself what I can learn from this experience, or what's another way I can look at this? Continue to engage in regular exercise activities, such as taking walks or finding your favorite exercise routine. This helps reduce stress and keep moods in line. Lastly, finding a support system, whether it be a meet-up group, walk group, friends, family, or a supportive social group.

- **Embrace Self-Care**

"Self-care is a necessity, not a luxury". Take an hour a day to do something for yourself, whether to schedule a massage, get your hair done, or eat healthy. This will help restore and rejuvenate you to help you with your day.

As I come to a close, I just want to remind you of what I shared so you can have a clear path forward. I shared my story early on in childhood with seeing toxic relationships and also experiencing them myself. I shared my story with you so you know who I am and that I have walked in this most of my life and know what you may be feeling. I talked about the transformation and reclaiming myself again. The climb back to self-empowerment and what that did for me. This is important to show you that even though the experience was horrible and tragic you too can overcome and still live a happy life. I was able to achieve professionally and personally and thrive. I talked about my entrepreneurship into coaching other women to heal from toxic relationships. This was very important to share with you my journey that led me here to help others and is my life purpose. Lastly, I shared with you five actionable items that you can take with you to help you start living an empowered life.

Remember the journey to healing and empowerment begins with a single step and holding yourself accountable. I encourage you to meet me at the next level to take a stand in your empowered life. I'm inviting you to join me on a discovery call or join my coaching program so we can work together to achieve your empowerment and personal development goals. You can connect with me on my website at coachjenniferw.com and workwithjenniferwallace.com. Socials are:

I will leave you with this: ***Rise Above and Reclaim you power!***

With much love, sending good vibes of empowerment and continued success on your personal development path, Coach Jennifer W (Jennifer Wallace)

***

To contact Jennifer:

www.coachjenniferw.com or www.workwithcoachjenniferw.com

Social Media:

Facebook: https://www.facebook.com/coachjenniferw

Instagram: https://www.instagram.com/coachjenniferw/

YouTube: https://www.youtube.com/@CoachJenniferW

LinkedIn: https://www.linkedin.com/company/coachjenniferw

Patrick Richard Garcia

Patrick Richard Garcia is a 1x international best-selling author, transformational & developmental strategist, results coach, learning disability champion, and owner of Hustle Revival Enterprises. He helps entrepreneurs to revive their hustle instincts through result-producing and intensive self-development activities simultaneously by aiming to accomplish life and business together.

He is also an inspirational speaker. On September 2023, Patrick competed on Speaker Slam: Empowerment and has drawn great attention on his speech dedicated to his learning disability story and encouraging his Filipino community to be inspired in seeking continuous growth. Patrick appeared on OMNI News – Filipino Edition to speak more in-depth on how his impact within his community and sharing his story will create the seeds of further grassroots work.

Thereon, he started his journey in further developing his craft in storytelling. Not only competing in competitions on and offline sharing his powerful story, but also on other platforms to inspire as many individuals with the similarities he has and accomplish more than the label of LD.

Patrick has been recognized by two magazines: Your Success and UnMasking Motivation for his extraordinary commitment to the business, entrepreneurship, and personal development space.

He currently resides in Toronto, ON, Canada and is married with his wife, Grace.

Embracing the Shift: A Journey of Personal Transformation

By Patrick Richard Garcia

The Catalyst: A Life of Unfulfilled Success

In 2019, I hit rock bottom. I was in debt; a dead-end job and my long-term relationship was nearing its end. I was not moving up within the company I was working for, and I felt my potential was limited with the opportunities given. I was also in rough physical shape and not treating my body well. I was overweight, working on empty all the time, not eating right, not exercising on a regular basis. I was working in a high-pressure environment I had artificially created with impossible expectations. I was working 70+ hour work weeks and had collected insurmountable debt from years of people-pleasing and missed out on countless family events and sacrificed precious memories. Something had to change.

The Awakening: Confronting the Discontent

I had been with the same partner for nearly seven years, but we had grown apart. Our plans for the future were not aligned. We saw financials very differently and had stopped spending quality time together because of schedule constraints. There were cultural standards that were conflicting with our own moral code, and it hindered our capabilities to grow as a couple. Lastly, we hadn't established a fundamental core value system, and a fulfilling relationship looked different for each of us. I did not foresee the end of the relationship earlier because I was desperately trying to save it - at the cost of my own being. She wanted more stability, a house, kids. I wanted that but needed to establish my career and a vision for my future.

I had no career ambitions at the time and was looking into more entrepreneurial endeavors. I researched multi-level marketing companies (known as network marketing, to build a business structure that allows the top percentage of individuals to gain the highest margins), I looked at opening a physical storefront business selling vehicles and was considering going back to school to study pharmacy and open pharmacies of my own. I saw myself being more giving and developing something for others to continue growing in their lives. I was not only looking for a passion to develop, but a purpose. Exploring entrepreneurship began with learning from T. Harv Eker. His teachings began with building a strong understanding of business financials and how to create something that aligned with my purpose, which was to have an impact on others so that we will thrive together and be successful wherever we go in life. Up until that point in my life, it had never felt like I was the driver in my own career. I was stuck in an employee environment with limited income and time.

In my current work, I was at the top of my pay scale and was seeking opportunities to move into a leadership role. The opportunities to be a lead, trainer, or supervisor was in the corporate ladder range. But it was not enough to get the position, I likely needed more experience and/or another company to take me in to give me a shot in leading a team. I also had bigger issues at hand: My health was deteriorating at a pace where if I didn't make some changes, it would lead to chronic issues and health complications. That created a strong sense of urgency, and I started by losing weight.

Over the course of three months in 2019, I changed my eating habits and lost 30 pounds. I began to enjoy my life again. But there was still something daunting hanging over my head–debt. I was still in a financially unstable place. I had been investing some of my income into self-development and mentorship, but I had also borrowed money with high interest rates. I had a lack of true understanding of how financials in my own country worked, in this case Canada, and I felt hopeless when my spending habits had increased debt and become larger than my income. There were moments where I couldn't sleep properly at night, constantly thinking about how I was going to fix this dire situation. My debt had become larger than my income.

I was under a vast amount of stress and my mental health was failing. This feeling negated any progress with weight loss and sustaining a new, healthier me. And I lost my inspiration to continue maintaining the hard work I put in to keep the weight as is. I fell into the people-pleasing and the voices of others in my life who encouraged me to stop the weight loss progress, which ironically was the one of the reasons to do so to prove others wrong. To find a solution, I researched and found debt management assistance programs. I sought assistance in getting my debt managed and I got approved for a consumer proposal to get nearly 75% of my debt written off with the rest being on an affordable payment plan.

The following are three actionable changes from that point in my life that led me to where I am today:

- Eat well. By making the best choices, one moment at a time. Taking your health for granted is an absolute disgrace to your only shot of living your life on this planet. If you plan to make a sacrifice to get a gain, it better be suited for a temporary amount of time.
- Don't have many "What If" thoughts. It is great to have them for fun discussions, as soon as it becomes more emotionally pact - it is time to stop. It will create regrets.
- Enjoy the process more. Whether it is discovering yourself, a partner you desire, etc. It is a marathon, not a sprint. As cliche as it goes.

The Leap: Transitioning to a New Path

I met my mentor Grant Cardone in November 2019, and he said something I will never forget. He mentioned to me very briefly - keep learning and 10X! I didn't understand what it meant at the time, but I bought his book called *The 10X Rule* to fully grasp it on a deeper level. One of the biggest learnings from the start was how to align myself with people who cared about others' successes. I just needed to be around a mentor who has been in my circumstances and desires to share their expertise and experience to fast track my advancement in life, whether in business, or other ventures. I went into it with the hope that my mentor could help me transform my thinking, override my operating system, and increase my perspective.

Over the next year, I attended various conferences I had always wanted to attend. One was a personal development conference called Archangel Summit in September 2019, and another was a wealth building conference called Wealth Hacking in November. The personal development was a great experience. I met with other fellow solopreneurs and friends; I even attended the pre-conference workshop as a VIP attendee. Seeing many people in one room, aiming for the same or similar objective - developing a mission that will impact and transform lives–was empowering. The wealth building session was another dynamic experience, learning about financial stability and creating wealth through many methods of investments, such as real estate, trading, and other business venture opportunities. I gained a whole new perspective on financial literacy, and realized, on a deeper level, how I'd gotten myself into a bad financial situation.

The first few months of 2020 were a period of deep introspection for me. With the global shutdown and my financial situation becoming dire with the debt management program I signed up for, I needed to learn how to strike and prepare for a long duration of inactivity. In addition to the mentorship, there were specialized skillset programs, such as business development, sales, marketing, leadership, and public speaking based on the type of package that was selected. I knew I needed them all, however I focused on sales, marketing, and public speaking first. Public speaking I had some experience, but not the extensive version where they go more in-depth about it and how to use it for new situations on a global scale. I had to trust their knowledge and their methods in order for me to move forward during a very difficult time. One of the programs I took more seriously was exploring and building stages of my own, in-person and virtually. Stages that are designed to expose your personal brand and business on the local and global scale. There were many ways on how to open them based on budget and client reach. I focused my time and energy on two of the most applicable ones: Virtual and podcast appearances as a guest.

Having the right mentorship to propel me forward, I needed to build some temporary cash flow to not only fund the mentorship and programs but get my business started. I applied to work as a custodian in the engineering department at Apotex, Inc. The inspiration to apply for the position came from the fact that I was using government assistance for four months and I started to get very comfortable, losing my work ethic in weeks. I quickly learned and adapted to the training plus learning new skills. A non-management position for a coordinator opened up and I applied. It was higher paying with more responsibilities and leading 50 custodians in the department.

The manager did a formal interview, and the supervisors were supportive of giving me this position. It was approved and I got started on February 2021. I was ecstatic. With the great pay and overtime came immense pressure to sustain targets for the department and myself. Leadership was a skill I'd always heard so many times in the classroom and volunteering, but to apply it in a workplace environment was a whole different story. I discovered that there are endless possibilities when there is a present opening, and I needed to take it. It was comfortable and uncomfortable because I created a false sense of limiting beliefs that were actually nonexistent.

At the same time, for the first time in my life, I felt extremely confident in my capabilities to lead a team while building my own skill sets. It was a positive breath of fresh air. With increased self-esteem and the eagerness and confidence to ask questions when I needed to feel good. Even trusting my superiors enough to share troubles at work and in my personal life felt good. I've never had such an environment that was encouraging and also reinforcing the right amount of toughness so they prepared me to ensure that individuals cannot walk over me, but rather build the respect from other coworkers and superiors in different departments. Due to our role in the department of engineering to maintain all cleanliness and maintain quality assurance standards, we needed to work together while not disrupting our own line of work.

My Learnings - How to take on new opportunities when it unexpectedly presents itself to you?

- To really adapt to pressure is taking on more responsibilities in a short period of time without much room to adjust rapidly. I noticed adaptations expand when it is given spontaneously and expectedly.
- Establishing core values and perspectives when you are selecting the right person to spend the rest of your life with.

Without that, it will be difficult to build upon that foundation.

- It is fundamentally sound to mention that readjusting and pivoting to a right set of circumstances can cause an effect of momentum building up to more great things, also known as the "Law of Attraction".
- By learning that growth can be in short spurts instead of years and years of development, it can be fast tracked when completed properly.

The Challenge: Navigating the Unknown

With all the experiences, learnings and knowledge that started to formulate my character and the environment I wanted to be in, I started to burn out. While working intense overtime hours in my coordinator position, I knew the kind of help I needed to be able to advance my entrepreneurial endeavors: I needed to "pay to play" to obtain the spotlight for a short period of time. It was challenging because it was the most frightening part to overcome and yet, the number one component that held me back was fear. I still was figuring out everything while being pulled into various directions. That is why having a mentor was crucial to stay within the community and be updated on current trends and knowledge. To be guided during the highs and lows of life and understanding how business transforms within months to a year - looking at how they transition.

I attended free virtual challenges and workshops held virtually, paying for the top package to book my dates strategically. There were sessions for sales, marketing, leadership, real estate and business exiting. Real estate was more about determining how I could leverage it while I start off rebuilding my financial situation and secure a plan moving forward. It was very difficult to move faster because my circle of influence was not large, being around negativity and the undesirability to accomplish big goals than themselves.

The beginning of 2022, I was back to facing the unknown in my professional life. I had left my position as coordinator and was determined to find a new opportunity that challenged me in a different way. I went back to my dead-end job to sustain myself financially and start a clean slate with the company. With my background and experience, along with the connection with management - it was seamless. I knew I was entering back into a familiar environment, however my perspective changed, and I respected my time more than ever. With just working for over a year, I decided to take a chance to apply for the first luxury brand private residences I worked for during the shutdown - The Residences at the Ritz Carlton, Toronto. This work allowed me to have more flexibility with my time and be involved more with my mentor; it was also a less stressful position. The staff and management appreciated my hard work ethic and determination to move over to their department. Despite being in a lower position than the previous one I had, the pay was slightly higher with less stress and responsibilities. It was a breath of fresh air as it took my focus and attention towards applying the knowledge of figuring out my next move.

It was hard to conceptualize everything because I didn't seek any guidance from anyone, I had to decide everything on my own. The mentorship component was a northern star concept I used to foresee the kind of future I desire. The future I look forward to is creating an empire with a wonderful woman, along with having great impactful children and the lifestyle that builds on stability and having the freedom to do whatever I desire at any given time. To start that process, I first need to get the required coaching to keep me under control. Definitely a distinguished difference between getting mentored versus getting coached. Getting mentored is learning all the knowledge and working on how to apply what they learn so you can figure out my own strengths and weaknesses. Coaching is putting it all together and executing it with someone to keep me accountable.

One of the tougher aspects of building a business is that many people are already doing them. The main industry I desired to be in was the coaching industry. Discovering this was my goal was merely me reflecting back on my own experiences and the person I was becoming. I reflected on the impact I felt I made in the places where I volunteered and worked, and knew I would make a great coach. I was drawn to the transformational and developmental side of coaching, bringing the short-term and long-term growth strategies together. But this decision making and pressure on myself was putting a lot of pressure on my mental health, also, and decision making around everyday things began to drain me.

The Breakthrough: Finding Success and Fulfillment

By mid-2022, the world was slowly opening up and I took the chance to attend my first in-person event in Miami, Florida. It was for a relationships mastermind workshop called 10X Relationships. I wanted to attend to grasp a better understanding on how to attract the right partner and also develop the right values on my end to be a great contributor for the relationship I desire. Prior to that, I was a contributing co-author for three books in the space of business and personal development. They were: (1) Our Yellow Brick Road, (2) Brand Sharks Vol. II, and a (3) Journey to Riches: Live Your Passion) The in-person event was for Relationship Mastery from my mentor's wife. She was hosting a two-day workshop, sharing her experience on how her and her husband truly learned how to develop a powerful empire as a couple. A remarkable chance to briefly chat with her and be a good contributing attendee in asking good questions to ensure I can maximize my learning. Following that, I attended a 2000+ in-person conference called 10X Growth Conference. My mentor was entering his 8th year hosting it in Las Vegas, Nevada. It was a great time, and my stay was nearly a week; I took the chance to explore the beautiful state as much I could while using it as a reflective time to see where my life was heading to.

The biggest breakthrough I took was taking on two public speaking competitions. The preparation for both of them was very intensive. Speaker Slam - Empowerment was the first one I heavily put emphasis on because it was my 1st live competition I ever did. I did all the workshops and shared my successes on social media. It was my time to shine and compete with the best speakers! I prepared intensely for it - memorizing, reciting it daily, and really made it feel as if it was my own piece of art. I got branding and coaching included, to really boost my personal brand and credibility as a speaker. With all that work, I did really well for my 1st ever speaking competition. With the feedback I got from my speaking coach, I was very joyful of how much I grew and became as a individual to get where I was.

The second speaking competition was from Merge Worldwide and it was held in Niagara Falls, Ontario, Canada. I knew the experience and meeting wonderful people was the energy and inspiration. I adjusted my speeches on the fly. Adjusting my speeches on the fly, I knew I had gained some skill to be strategic with this competition. I received encouraging feedback. I was growing toward alignment with my goal of becoming a transformational & developmental coach to others. With this success, I looked into being on bigger stages and eventually to work with more high net worth clients that strive for results.

Overall, having these two speaking engagements really elevated my confidence when I was able to put the right framework in place to become a better speaker - it also, in turn, improved my fundamental everyday communication skills in any surrounding. Communication has been a constant skill I needed to work on since I was a child, and it drastically affected how I interacted with many different kinds of people in all walks of life. It has even influenced how I maintain relationships and friendships, and even understand how to initiate first contact and the proper way of conversing personally and professionally. With a solid vision of my future, I have been able to take advantage of opportunities along the way and grow faster.

The Integration: Creating a Balanced and Purposeful Life

With my new relationship (engaged and now married in a span of a year!) being integrated with everything I do, everything else fell into place. We met online on Hinge last March 2023 with a language barrier. She was from Vietnam arriving as a student and in the beginning, it was challenging to talk to one another. Despite that, we continued to get to know one another and became an exclusive couple. It felt right because we knew what we wanted, we had similar common values and goals, and we both strived to be the best version of ourselves. My wife supports my best interests and vice versa. We listen to each other's opinions and ideas. What was different in this relationship was the aura and energy we displayed together. We had the target to find ways on how to communicate openly and improve on it. And we weren't afraid to share our insecurities and secrets with each other. It was based on intentionality and purpose; it didn't feel forceful.

In my position as an Overnight Residences Valet at the Residences at the Ritz-Carlton Toronto, it's been two years, and I am looking into moving up to a managerial role - also being a security guard opened up many opportunities for me. I will be putting more focus in the security industry due to the growing demand and the avenues that open up for greater growth. It is related to my entrepreneurial endeavors because I had looked into opening up my own security company and improving it from the ground up to become a competitive business owner in providing an essential service in today's market. With all the blessings that are coming through, I thank my new mentor JT Foxx for believing in me. He personally coached me and as well has been leaning towards his ideology and learning curve in how he became a multi-millionaire at a very young age. Everything feels different from being more calculating in my decisions and choices. I need to do my risk benefit analysis on all of them to feel confident that the benefits and risk involved outweigh the consequences that could potentially be more dangerous than good.

The Legacy: Reflecting on the Journey

This has been a five-year journey. The vision I had for myself was always expanding, but at times it was constantly reverting back to thinking small. The concept of thinking small was triggering, but when I think about it in-depth, thinking small was hindering me in taking steps forward. However, having a more definitive goal and thinking in small steps rather than small perspectives, I have been able to shift and break through old ways of thinking, and reshape how I see the world. I have also been able to grow in my interactions with other people and see how I can either help them or allow them to be part of the tribe I am creating. I believe that accomplishing bigger things for others than myself became a recurring theme. I enjoy giving back to the communities that have served me and to other organizations that I have been a part of in relation to business and personal development. It is a great honor that I will be a philanthropist to provide others with the greatness that they see for themselves.

***

To contact Patrick:

Business # 437-236-5774

Facebook: www.facebook.com/patrickrichardgarcia

Instagram: @theofficialpatrickrgarcia

LinkedIn: https://www.linkedin.com/in/patrickrichardgarcia/

Lynn McIntosh

Lynn McIntosh helps men and women regain their confidence and thrive after leaving a toxic relationship.

Lynn is both a certified coach and hypnotist with several years of experience dealing with narcissistic personalities. She is a co-author of two #1 international best-selling books on empowering women to success, was nominated Woman of Inspiration Canada 2020, will be speaking at the 21st Century Women's Entrepreneurship, Positive Psychology and Wellness Summit in November in Valencia, Spain, was selected Coach of the Year in her respective niche by the "Rise to Greater Heights Network, has been invited to do a Ted Talk, attended conferences on narcissism in Dallas, Texas and Hollywood and has appeared on several podcasts.

Through personal coaching programs, her clients release their negative emotions, anger, sadness, frustration, and loneliness and learn how to regain their confidence and sense of self-worth to move forward into a joyful life.

A resident of Toronto, Ontario, Lynn loves to speak and is available to do interviews on subjects such as overcoming toxic relationships, dealing with narcissistic personalities, and increasing personal confidence.

FROM RAGS TO RICHES

By Lynn McIntosh

Telling my story can be difficult but very healing at the same time. Being a victim of narcissistic abuse can happen to anyone. When it happens to you, you feel isolated, invisible, unheard, like you are the only one going through this. You can't choose your future.

I had a very happy childhood. My father was an airline captain for Air Canada, and my mother owned her own fashion/clothing business. As a family, we had traveled to England and Scotland, skied in Austria, Switzerland, Denmark, the Caribbean, Florida many times, and California. In my younger years, my mother and I were close. I had one younger sister. My mother would take me shopping, over to her friend's house, teach me to cook and bake, introduce me to ballet and jazz. I still love dancing. She also introduced me to modeling. I, myself, did love to dance and did love the fashion world, not needing my mother's influence. I think it was naturally born in me.

When I turned fifteen, I met my first boyfriend. He was a great guy, and we were best friends and lovers. He played half-back on the football team and played trumpet in the school band. He was perfect in my eyes. In the two and one-half years we went out, we fought once. We were madly in love for being so young. Many of our friends were also couples; there were parties, proms, and football games. There was school, too, of course, but I was blessed to have a wonderful first boyfriend and good friends at school.

I was very young, and after two years, my parents thought I needed to spread my wings a little, date other boys, and experience life on my own for a while. The pressure was put on me, and at the end of Grade 12, we split up. Back then, in Canada, we had Grade 13, and he and I never got back together.

One year after high school finished, I found myself feeling lost and confused. Unsure of a career, I went to college for one year. After college, I fell into a deep depression, still suffering from the loss of the relationship I had in high school. My mother didn't understand why I was feeling this way. I think it was a lack of empathy and also wounds she had from her childhood that were never examined and thus healed. This made her insensitive to my situation. I moved to my grandmother's, but she was not functioning properly. Depressed, I would lie around for days at a time, just getting up to eat or go to the lady's room. Being 20, you are supposed to enjoy life, go to school or work, have parties, and have new experiences. Instead, I was on a couch, feeling hopeless and gloomy.

My father came to my rescue, and he suggested I take the Dale Carnegie Course. I needed self-confidence and also needed to vent my emotions and feelings. I agreed. That course changed my life in my 20s. I completed the course and even went back a second time, taking on the role of assistant coach, helping new members as I had once done a year earlier.

My confidence was healthy, I was happy, and I felt motivated again. At 25, I got hired by a big corporate company, the Canadian Standards Association. I bought my first car, experienced dating, met new people, and matured as all this happened. I was walking on a cloud, experiencing life as a single woman and having the time of my life.

When I was 30 I met my future husband. We met at a dance, started dating and in 2 years we were married. We had two children, and I thought everything was going great.

Giving is hard. Giving is victimhood. Giving makes me weak. I want to take you back to the early 2000s. I was married with young children, 3 and 5 years old. We had a beautiful home in Bolton, Ontario, Canada, and I was happy to be home raising children. I had worked for many years and needed a break from corporate life.

Like everyone, I wanted a loving relationship that made me feel good about myself. My marriage started off well. We were happy enjoying our life in our new home with our young children.

Unfortunately, my husband was a narcissist. A narcissist is someone who insists on having the best of everything - the best car, the best suit, the best phone. They are always envious of others and believe others envy them. My ex-husband would monopolize conversations and exaggerate his achievements and talents. He became very selfish and wasn't always there for me.

He was very grandiose and had a sense of entitlement. His narcissistic traits were hidden. His mannerisms hinted at condescension and disapproval. He expected everything from everyone else and gave nothing of himself. What I found was that I was constantly giving of myself with no appreciation, only expectations of more giving.

Now, the reason I'm telling you this is not to complain but to show you what a narcissistic personality is like. Some of you may be living with a narcissist and don't even know it.

As a result, I was miserable, and worse, I had developed a victim's mindset. I felt compelled to give my energy to someone who was essentially a vampire. Taking…taking…taking and seldom giving back. I felt powerless, and it seemed I had no choice but to be in this situation.

There was someone in my life who was totally the opposite of my dad. He was a kind and generous man. Giving wasn't a dirty word to him. I took his death really hard. He was the guiding light in my life. And then he died. This pushed me to feel hopeless, helpless, and lonely.

So my dad was gone, and I started to party to forget my pain. I would go out to my favorite place, meet friends, and have a couple of glasses of wine. There was karaoke and a dance band where you could dance until you dropped. This party life was prevalent in my life. I wanted to escape the pain of divorce and death, and when I went out for that few hours on Friday night, I could forget the pain and find comfort in music, friends, and wine.

After a couple of months, a light came on. How could I change? I was in a downward spiral; if something didn't shift, my life would not look pretty. My first thought was I had to get out of my victim mentality. Giving and giving in to my ex-husband had been painful. How could I do this? How could I shift the focus from myself to others?

Suddenly, a light came on. Maybe giving wasn't the problem; it was the solution.

I had been giving to the wrong person—to someone who didn't appreciate it. I gave and gave without getting anything back, feeling invisible and unimportant. But what if I gave like my father did—to those in need without any expectation? I decided to try it.

There was a center in town that supplied food to families in need. That day, I decided to drive up to the grocery store and buy food that families would enjoy. I walked through the aisles and felt good. Oh, a jar of pasta sauce, a can of tomato soup, a package of pasta.

I bought the food, put it in the car, and as I drove to the center, I had a great feeling of anticipation. I walked into the center with the four grocery bags and handed them to the receptionist with a smile, saying I would like to donate the food. She said, thank you so much. We greatly appreciate it. I drove away with a huge smile on my face, feeling so good. The next week, I received an email thanking me for my contribution and saying that a family enjoyed the food. It was such a feeling of satisfaction. I got acknowledgment for helping people, and most of all, I helped a family in need.

That experience made me realize there was a huge difference between giving to someone as a victim and giving by choice. Giving as a victim is a never-ending process, and you get nothing in return, but giving by choice is very empowering. And I have taken that powerful sense of giving beyond others to myself in the form of personal development and self-care. In the past few years, I have studied the power of positive thinking and the subconscious mind. I feel positive and excited about life. I swim 3x per week, which keeps me uplifted. I recognize giving to myself is as powerful as giving to others. And part of that giving was learning. I now recognize giving is easy, giving is powerful, and giving makes you strong.

I've spoken of my mother and my ex-husband. Now, there is the subject of my good friend. The three closest relationships in my life were all with narcissists! She was the third narcissist.

Ann and I met in 1985 when we were both working at the Canadian Standards Association. We clicked, and both being single and in our 20's, would enjoy going out to dances, ski trips, and social occasions. Having lots of fun, meeting and dating men, having cars and good jobs, we were having the time of our lives. After seven years, in 1992, we both got married and went our separate ways. Then, in 2006, a mutual friend arranged for Ann and I to meet again. We enjoyed going out socially, to see bands, dance, and party. She was a good singer, and I was a dancer when I was younger, so we each had no problem having fun. I was raising my ten-year-old and eight-year-old at the time. I was a single mom; my ex would be there if I needed him, but I was raising them and was doing the best I could.

Six months into our renewed relationship, I noticed my friend enjoyed her wine. When I arrived at her house, she would have a drink in hand, and when we went out, some nights, she would have one too many. I thought maybe she was just stressed at her job and was letting off steam. Then I noticed on our Thursday night phone calls she would be drunk again. I began to realize she had a drinking problem.

One night, we were out at a social event, and a friend of ours asked me to dance. When we finished the dance, I sat down, and she turned to me and shouted, "Why are you dancing with him? You have a boyfriend." "What's your problem?" Everyone in the room heard her, and I sat there, wanting to climb under the table. Then I thought, I'm not doing this; I got up and left. When I got in my car, I was dumbfounded. What just happened? Then my phone rang. It was our friend who I had danced with, and he said: "Come back." "Everything is ok." "She is outside talking to friends. "Come back and enjoy yourself." I said, "No, Chris, I'm leaving." "I'm not going to be subject to that kind of abuse."

It was Christmas 2019, and the owners of a restaurant/bar had invited me to the Christmas party the week before. When I walked into the venue, laughter and music were blaring. Everyone was in Christmas cheer. Then I saw my friend walk up to me. Guess what? Drunk again. She blurted out, "What are you doing here?" "Shouldn't you be home with your kids?" The whole room turned their heads to look at us. I thought, oh no, she is doing this again. I said, "Ann, you need help." "What is wrong with you?" "Calm down." "I was invited to this party." "Excuse me." I walked down to a table of three ladies I knew and sat down. I joined in with the conversation. All of a sudden, a chair was dragged up beside me, and down sat my drunk friend. She said, "Why are you here?" "Why don't you go home to your kids?" I was angry, but at the same time, I was sad. I had seen my friend transform into a controlling, jealous narcissist with a drinking problem. It was sad to see someone who used to laugh, be social, friendly, intelligent, and kind turn into a loser. How do you help someone like this? You can't. Only they can help themselves. My friend died of alcohol poisoning in 2022.

Having relationships with people you love who are narcissistic is a painful experience. Yes, there are a lot of good times, but these relationships can also leave you drained, and you may lose your sense of self. You feel isolated because you are so ensnared in the narcissist web that you don't see outside of it, and you feel like you are the only one this is happening to. You freeze up because you feel helpless. A pattern of devaluation and criticism can leave you with very little self-esteem and confidence.

Gaslighting tactics make you doubt your decision-making abilities. Narcissists blame you, even for their mistakes. Their rageful attacks make you believe you can't do anything right. You might notice appetite changes, stomach pain, and fatigue. You feel restless and unsettled; you don't recognize yourself; you have trouble setting boundaries, and you have symptoms of anxiety and depression. I experienced all this, each at different times.

One day, I had an epiphany, got angry, and decided to start the healing process. I had a happy childhood, and I knew what happiness was. I started researching the power of positive thinking, practicing gratitude, doing acts of kindness, and practicing self-hypnosis. All this helped me to heal. Working with the subconscious mind, getting out of my own way by helping others and thinking positively, and looking at what I had in my life versus what I didn't have were practices that slowly changed my mindset and my self-esteem. I also took up swimming, which releases endorphins in the brain and makes you feel good. Doing all this every day, gradually, my joy and love for life returned.

Successful people started noticing what I was doing, and they invited me to events where I would speak on stage and network with other business owners. I took a small course with Adam Mortimer, a coach for Eric Worre, a famous network marketer. He said I would make a great coach, being a good listener, authentic, and knowledgeable about narcissism. I obtained my coaching certification. So, I didn't go looking to be a coach; coaching found me. It was fate, meant to be.

I know the pain of narcissistic abuse, and I knew back then I could help a lot of people. Taking people from confusion and sadness to joy has always been a passion of mine. Now, I get to do something I love and am passionate about. My clients, when completing my 3-month program, are whole, have healthy self-confidence and a direction in their lives, are motivated, and have self-worth and dignity. I have found my purpose, or maybe it found me. There is no greater gift you can give or receive than to honor your calling. It's why you were born. And how you become most truly alive.

***

To contact Lynn:

facebook.com/lynn.mcintosh.1612

www.linkedin.com/in/lynn-mcintosh

YouTube: Lynn McIntosh Relationship Expert

Afterword

Life is always a series of transitions… people, places and things that shape who we are as individuals. Often, you never know that the next catalyst for change is around the corner.

Jim Britt and Jim Lutes have spent decades influencing individuals to blossom into the best version of themselves.

Allow all you have read in this book to create introspection and redirection if required. It's your journey to craft.

The Change is a series. A global movement. Watch for future releases and add them to your collection. If you know of anyone who would like to be considered as a co-author for a future book, have them email our offices at support@jimbritt.com.

The individual and combined works of Jim Britt and Jim Lutes have filled seminar rooms to maximum capacity and created a worldwide demand.

The blessings go both ways as Jim and Jim are always willing students of life. Out of demand for life-changing programs and events, Jim and Jim conduct seminars worldwide.

To Schedule Jim Britt or Jim Lutes as your featured speaker at your next convention or special event, email Jim Britt at: support@jimbritt.com or Jim Lutes at: mindpowerpro@yahoo.com

For more info on Jim & Jim visit: www.LutesInternational.com or www.JimBritt.com

For information on Jim Britt's online coaching course Cracking the Rich Code: http://CrackingTheRichCode.com

Master your moment as they become hours that become days.

Do something remarkable today! Your legacy awaits.

Blessings,

Jim Britt and Jim Lutes

www.facebook.com/jimluteshttps://mindmotionacademy.com

www.ingramcontent.com/pod-product-compliance
Lightning Source LLC
LaVergne TN
LVHW021804060526
838201LV00058B/3234

* 9 7 9 8 3 3 0 5 5 1 0 1 9 *